W0035637

VAMPIRE STORIES

Love Until Dawn

Gina Billy

© 2010 Compact Verlag GmbH München
Alle Rechte vorbehalten. Nachdruck, auch auszugsweise,
nur mit ausdrücklicher Genehmigung des Verlages gestattet.
Redaktion: Helga Aichele
Fachredaktion: Alison Frankland
Produktion: Wolfram Friedrich
Typographischer Entwurf: EKH Werbeagentur GbR, textum GmbH
Umschlaggestaltung: EKH Werbeagentur GbR
Titelabbildungen: www.Fotolia.com: Elwynn, Forgiss, Julien Gremillot

ISBN: 978-3-8174-8261-0
2010 2011 2012 2013 2014   10 9 8 7 6 5 4 3 2 1

www.compactverlag.de

Vorwort

Liebe Leserin, lieber Leser,

so packend war Englisch lernen noch nie! Diese Vampire Story kombiniert romantische Hochspannung mit dem bewährten didaktischen Konzept der Compact Lernlektüren.

Das vorliegende Buch wurde speziell für Lernende der Stufe C1 des Europäischen Referenzrahmens konzipiert. Vokabelerklärungen direkt auf der Seite erleichtern das Lesen. Jedes Kapitel wird durch abwechslungsreiche Übungen ergänzt, die auf unterhaltsame Weise Wortschatz, Textverständnis und Grammatik trainieren und festigen. Infokästen weisen auf sprachliche und grammatikalische Besonderheiten hin. Alle Vokabeln können Sie im Glossar noch einmal nachschlagen.

Viel Spaß und Erfolg beim
Englisch lernen mit Biss!

Die Ereignisse und die handelnden Personen in diesem Buch sind frei erfunden. Etwaige Ähnlichkeiten mit tatsächlichen Ereignissen oder lebenden Personen wären rein zufällig und unbeabsichtigt.

Inhalt

Zu diesem Buch

In einer Höhle in den Waliser Bergen findet die Vampirin Arianne
Zuflucht vor dem Morgengrauen. Zu spät bemerkt sie, dass auch
der verletzte Gareth in dieser Höhle Unterschlupf gesucht hat.
Nicht nur sein Blut ist eine große Versuchung – der attraktive
Amerikaner weckt auch Gefühle in ihr, die sie lange vergessen
glaubte.
Als plötzlich Ariannes Erzfeind auftaucht, muss sie mit Gareth
im Schlepptau fliehen. Kann sie ihn beschützen? Und wie wird
Gareth reagieren, wenn er die Wahrheit über sie erfährt?

1 Dawn's Temptation

With a mixed sigh of relief and regret, Arianne raised her eyes from the remains of her meal on the forest ground. Licking the last drop delicately from the corner of her mouth, she lifted her head to the trees above, threw back the hood of her cape and let her long, straight hair flow freely down her back. Suddenly, she realized that the storm had weakened. No more rain, and with shock she saw that the night was almost over. A glimmer of light was dancing on a wild flower in the clearing ahead.

Oh, bloody hell, Arianne, you've done it again, she scolded herself. After all these years, she still hadn't learnt to keep better track of the time. Well, this was definitely not the moment for self-reflection. She needed to take cover.

It was past dawn, and just her luck, it looked as if it was going to be a clear, sunny day. There was not enough time to reach the car and drive to her cottage in a village near Cardiff. She had only minutes left to find a dark place before the sun reached her. She could not afford to take that risk. Quickly re-covering her hair, she fished out her sunglasses from the cloak's deep pocket, put them on and began to run with effortless strides.

delicately	sachte, auf zarte Weise
clearing	Lichtung
to scold	schimpfen
↯ just sb.'s luck	Pech gehabt!
effortless	leicht, mühelos
stride	großer Schritt

Miles away at her home, the garden gate was silently pushed open, even though nobody appeared to have touched it. A split second later, the front door knob seemed to turn all by itself and two shadows glided towards the door.

"Frederick, stop," whispered a female voice. "What if she's heard us?"

sister-in-law	Schwägerin
scent	Duft
mate	*hier*: Gefährtin, Partnerin
seductive	verführerisch
encroaching	sich aus-breitend

"My dearest Maegan," came the reply, "no one, not even Arianne, can hear me. And, my sweet, there's no need to worry. She is not here."

"Not here? But, Frederick, my love, how can that be? Have we come to the wrong place? You were so certain that our search was finally over."

"We were not mistaken, Meagan. Your **sister-in-law** does live here. I can smell her presence, but the **scent** is hours old, so apparently she's, well, out for the day."

A flash of anger appeared briefly in Frederick's eyes as he looked at his **mate**.

"And what shall we do now?" she asked.

"We will wait, Maegan. After over 13 decades, what's one more day to us? And, besides, I know exactly how we can pass the hours until Arianne returns to this place she calls home."

With a **seductive** smile, Frederick took Meagan's cool hand in his and led her through the now-open door into the hiding place she had hoped never to see.

The opening to the cave was so small that even Arianne's extraordinary power of sight almost missed it. Her flight through the forest had been thrilling. She had run at incredible speed, constantly on the lookout for a place to escape the **encroaching** sunlight. And then, out of the corner of her eye, she had seen the tiny cave with its promise of protection. With one last powerful leap, she reached the overhanging rocks and swept inside, just as the sun rose over the mountain.

"That was close, way too close," she told herself and vowed never, ever to let time get away from her again.

Smoothing her cloak, she began to have a look at her surroundings.

leap	Sprung, Satz
to sweep	*hier*: gleiten
to vow	geloben
decay	Fäulnis, Verfall
whiff	Hauch, Spur
hiss	Zischen
tempting	verlockend, verführerisch
trained on	gerichtet auf
to flutter	flattern
captivating	faszinierend, bezaubernd
ravishing	hinreißend, atemberaubend

The cave was much bigger than it had appeared from the outside. Its narrow entrance quickly widened into a roomier space, which, in turn, flowed into what seemed to be a type of tunnel. The cave smelt strange, though. Arianne identified dampness, decay, the smell of stones and there, a whiff of something familiar, something exciting.

A hiss escaped her slightly parted lips, and her dark-blue eyes began to turn silver. The tempting smell, so sweet, the one she had fought so long and hard to resist seemed to fill all her senses.

And then, she saw him.

Arianne stood stock still, her eyes trained on the sleeping man in the back corner of the cave. Clearly, he was still alive. She could see his muscular chest rising and falling. His eyelids fluttered and she heard him moan softly in his sleep. Then she saw the source of the captivating, ravishing scent. There, on his leg, was an improvised bandage drenched in blood.

Übung 1: Synonyms. Welche Begriffe haben dieselbe Bedeutung? Ordnen Sie zu!

1. ☐ incredible   a) approaching
2. ☐ vow   b) inviting
3. ☐ encroaching   c) unbelievable
4. ☐ decay   d) promise
5. ☐ tempting   e) decomposition

In the darkness of the cave in the Brecon Beacons National Park, Gareth Richards **groaned** in pain as he regained consciousness. One by one, the memories of the day and night before returned to his **fuzzy** brain. Shaking his head, he cautiously placed a hand on the source of his pain: a deep cut on his right leg.

Okay, good, the bleeding has slowed, he thought, but man, the wound hurts like hell. How could I have been so stupid as to slip on wet leaves, of all things, and then have the incredible bad luck to cut my leg wide open on a sharp stone?

to groan	stöhnen
fuzzy	*hier*: benommen, benebelt
to pass out	ohnmächtig werden
⚡ bum leg (US)	kaputtes Bein

Touching the wound again, Gareth remembered how he had somehow managed to crawl into the cave, cleanse the deep cut with some of his drinking water and bandage it with a handkerchief. Cold, exhausted and hurting, he must have **passed out**.

Closing his eyes once more, he wondered what he was going to do now. How was he going to manage to walk out of the wilderness with this **bum leg** and find help?

What on earth possessed me to go on a hiking tour in Wales anyway? I should have stayed home in the relative civilization of Hollywood, or at least have had the good sense to bring my mobile phone with me, he thought before falling into a restless slumber once more.

Übung 2: Past tense forms. Lesen Sie weiter und setzen Sie die korrekte Verbform ein!

Arianne **1.** sense _____ that the man **2.** go

_____ back to sleep and **3.** know _____

that he **4.** not see _____ her. Against her will,

she silently **5.** begin _____ to glide towards him.

Just one tiny little sip, just one, and then I will stop, Arianne told herself. He's alone and he's asleep, he won't even notice.

Her silent footsteps stopped as she reached the man lying helplessly on the cave's floor. Very slowly, she knelt beside him and reached out to touch the ultimate temptation. Her fingertips caressed the still-damp bandage, and she shuddered with longing.

"Hey! Who the hell are you and what are you doing?"

The angry words broke through Arianne's trance, and she withdrew her fingers, reluctantly wiping the trace of blood on the bottom of her red velvet skirt.

Gareth tried to see the figure in front of him more clearly. He had woken up with a start at the touch of delicate fingers on his throbbing leg.

slumber	Schlummer
to caress	streicheln, liebkosen
longing	Sehnsucht, Verlangen
reluctantly	widerwillig
throbbing	pochend

to muffle	dämpfen
rugged features *pl*	markante Gesichtszüge
tinged with	mit einer Spur von
untamed	wild, ungebändigt

I must be dreaming, he thought, or perhaps I injured my head in the fall as well.

The bit of daylight coming into the cave revealed a woman bent over his lower body. She was wearing some sort of hooded cape that partially covered her face and muffled her words as she finally spoke.

"I am Arianne, Arianne Gwynn," she answered as calmly as she could. "I was just about to remove your bandage and um, well, examine your injury. It looks as if you have suffered a nasty cut."

Arianne turned her eyes away from the man's leg and focused on his face. It was a sight worth seeing. He was not classically handsome, but possessed rugged features, sensual lips and chocolate-brown eyes tinged with glints of gold. His full head of black hair was on the curly side and gave him a bit of an untamed look. Oddly enough, she had the impression that she had seen him somewhere before. This feeling of recognition was followed by yet another strange thought. She found herself wondering what it would be like to kiss him.

Übung 3: True or false? Kreuzen Sie die richtigen Aussagen an!

1. Arianne hopes that Gareth hasn't seen her. ❑

2. Gareth is in pain when he wakes up. ❑

3. Gareth can hear Arianne clearly. ❑

4. Arianne recognizes Gareth from a past encounter. ❑

Amazed at herself, Arianne focused on the practical.

"Now it's your turn: Who are you and what happened to you?"

Gareth could finally see the woman now facing him, and her beauty took his breath away and left him momentarily speechless. Her eyes were huge pools of deep blue and had an unusual silver tinge. They were shining out of the palest face he had ever seen. Her ruby-red lips were slightly trembling beneath a perfect nose and above a gently rounded chin.

As she felt his eyes moving over her face and body, Arianne raised both her hands and slowly brushed the hood away, revealing her long, ebony-coloured hair that reached

ebony	*hier*: tiefschwarz
teasing	aufreizend, neckend
⚡ Has the cat got your tongue?	Hat es dir die Sprache verschlagen?
enchantress	bezaubernde Frau, Zauberin

well below her slim waist. At his obvious admiration, she gave him the full benefit of a teasing smile.

"Well, stranger, has the cat got your tongue?"

"No, but I think an enchantress has, or perhaps a fairy or, hopefully, a good witch. My name is Gareth Richards. I'm from the States and here on a hiking tour. As to what happened, that's a long story, but the short version is, I fell and hurt myself during the storm yesterday afternoon. I was able to make it into this cave, and – amazingly enough – you were at my side when I opened my eyes. And speaking of which, how is it that you happen to be here in this cave?"

"Um, well, that is an even longer story, Gareth. I was also out hiking in the park's Black Mountains, managed to wander about too long and ended up getting lost," she improvised.

Gareth thought her outfit was a bit odd for a hike in the Black Mountains, but maybe going hiking in a skirt and cape was some sort of strange custom in Wales.

"By the way, are you Welsh?" he asked, curious about this **dazzling** woman, who seemed to have appeared out of nowhere.

"Yes, I am. But we call ourselves Cymry in our native language."

"Yes, I know," he replied. "I may be an ignorant American, but my **ancestors** are from Wales, or Cymru if you prefer, and I did a bit of research before coming here for my vacation, I mean holiday."

dazzling	umwerfend, blendend
ancestors *pl*	Vorfahren

Arianne had to smile at his quick change to the British English word.

Übung 4: Vocabulary quiz. Enträtseln Sie das Lösungswort!

1. Arianne ... herself for forgetting the time.
   _ ☐ _ _ _ _

2. Brightly shining, fascinating.
   _ ☐ _ _ _ _ _ _

3. I don't know anything about it, I'm ... of it.
   _ _ _ _ ☐ _ _ _

4. The opposite of tanned.
   _ _ _ ☐

5. Arianne has a slim one.
   _ _ _ ☐ _

6. To Arianne, Gareth's blood smells...
   _ _ _ _ ☐ _ _ _

Lösung: ☐ ☐ ☐ ☐ ☐ ☐

"And what do you do when you are not **traipsing** around your ancestral lands, Gareth?" her curiosity **got the better of her**.

Gareth laughed and then tried to hide his surprise at [i] her question. Normally, he was recognized immediately every time he put his foot out of the door. I must really **look the worse for wear**, he thought.

Während man im Deutschen seine Über-raschung **über** etwas aus-drückt, wird das englische Substantiv **surprise** mit der Präposition **at** ergänzt.

⚡ to traipse	latschen
to get the better of sb.	die Oberhand über jmd. gewinnen
⚡ to look the worse for wear	lädiert aussehen

"Um, well, actually I'm an actor, in films. Perhaps you've seen one of them?"

Of course, she thought, that's why he seemed so familiar. What a bizarre coincidence.

"Yes, I should have known it immediately," she answered his question. "Certainly, I've seen your films. Who hasn't? But at the moment, I feel as if I have stumbled into a film myself."

Before he could ask her what she did for a living, Arianne quickly changed the subject by asking how his leg was doing.

"It still hurts, but I think the bleeding has stopped. By the way, do you think you could finish what you were doing before I woke up?"

"What!? Oh, you mean the bandage."

Arianne had to find an excuse to avoid that tempting situation. "I think you can manage to take it off yourself. I tend to, well, get a bit weak in the knees at the sight of blood, and besides, I wouldn't want to hurt you."

Gareth thought he actually wouldn't mind a bit of pain if it meant feeling the touch of her graceful hands on any part of his body.

"Okay, if I can't tempt you, then here goes."

13

to yank off	(ruckartig) abreißen
mesmerized	gebannt, wie hypnotisiert
to crave sth.	etw. begehren
gaze	Blick
⚡ to be out for the count	k.o. sein (bewusstlos)
intoxicating	berauschend

With one quick pull, he yanked off the bandage before Arianne had a chance to turn her head. The wound immediately began bleeding again. She stared mesmerized as the blood began to run down his leg and knew that this time, she would not be able to resist its call.

Occupied with trying to stop the fresh flow, Gareth did not see how Arianne's teeth were growing longer and sharper. The silver glow in her eyes began to intensify again as she slowly moved closer towards him and the substance that she craved.

"Arianne, I think I need your help. I know you said you can't stand the sight of blood, but could you please..."

Gareth's words suddenly stopped as he realized that Arianne was standing directly above him. He had not heard her move and as he looked up, he immediately noticed that her eyes were no longer blue at all and her teeth, oh my god, her teeth...

"Don't be afraid, Gareth," she whispered. "I am going to help you, really."

With that, she placed one hand gently on his knee and looked him directly in the eyes. As he stared into her silvery gaze, Gareth felt himself getting dizzy and sleepy at the same time. Although his heart was racing with fear, he somehow had the feeling that he was dreaming again. He could no longer keep his eyes open. I hope this is a movie, he thought before passing out.

The moment Gareth was out for the count, Arianne placed her lips on the bleeding wound and let out a sigh of pleasure. She had not drunk from a human since that first awful year in 1875, and the taste of Gareth's blood was absolutely intoxicating.

keep   struggle   sense   feast   control   instincts

It was like sipping the darkest, most delicious of red wines, and the bouquet threatened to make her lose **1.** _____. Arianne's head told her that she had to stop; otherwise, she would be unable to **2.** _____ the promise she had made to Gareth. Her **3.** _____, though, urged her to keep drinking, to enjoy the **4.** _____ in front of her until the very last drop. It was a hard inner **5.** _____, but somehow her common **6.** _____ took over.

Carefully, Arianne licked the edges of the wound one last time. Then with her **fangs**, she quickly bit her own wrist and let the **ensuing** drops of blood drip into the deep cut on Gareth's leg. As if by magic, the wound began to close.

Well, at least I can still use my powers to heal, she thought. Gareth was still unconscious, and with any luck, he would remain so for several hours. She just hoped her plan was going to work.

"Oh darling, you were as wonderful as ever," Maegan **purred** and kissed Frederick on the tip of his nose.

"Stop it, Maegan, you know how much I hate such human-like gestures."

fang	Reißzahn
ensuing	(nach)folgend
to purr	schnurren

15

"But Frederick, I just want to show you how much you mean to me and how I love being in bed with you, even if this bed does belong to Arianne."

At the sound of that name, Frederick let out an angry growl. How he had adored her. He had chosen her, turned her against her will into the creature she now was. He had given her the great honour of taking her as his mate. And then, she had deserted him and left him alone with only Maegan at his side. For this reason, Arianne must die.

Maegan noticed that Frederick's thoughts were no longer with her and let out a growl of her own. She knew he was obsessing about Arianne again, and her jealousy got the better of her.

Raising her voice, Maegan ordered Frederick to stop thinking about her rival for his affections. "You belong solely to me now, and I won't have you bringing her into bed with us. Oh Frederick, why can't you just forget her and let us go home and be happy together?"

Frederick knew he had to calm Maegan down; after all, he needed her to complete his revenge.

"I'm sorry, my love, but I cannot be totally at peace until Arianne has suffered and paid for what she did. Don't you think so, too, dearest?"

"Well, Frederick, I suppose you're right. It's just I sometimes think we could just forget about her running away and let her be."

Gathering her courage, she asked, "Am I not enough for you, Frederick?"

No, you're not, he wanted to say, but thought better of it. "You're everything I could ever want, Maegan, and as soon as Arianne is no longer on this earth, I will do all that I can to prove it to you."

Frederick caressed her cheek and placed his lips against her ear. "It won't be much longer now, my love. In just an hour or so, it will be **dusk**, and we can expect Arianne's return any time after the sun has set."

Sighing, Maegan sank into his arms. She knew that she had little time left to make her decision. Thinking about what she was going to do, she failed to see the look of hatred in Frederick's eyes or his **wicked** smile.

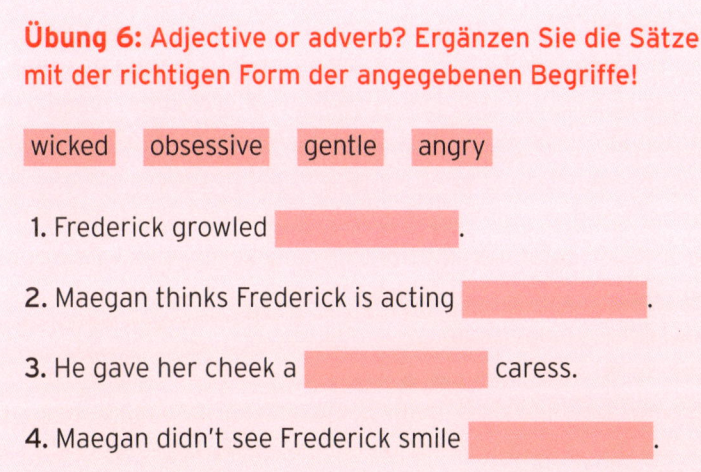

Übung 6: Adjective or adverb? Ergänzen Sie die Sätze mit der richtigen Form der angegebenen Begriffe!

wicked   obsessive   gentle   angry

1. Frederick growled _____.

2. Maegan thinks Frederick is acting _____.

3. He gave her cheek a _____ caress.

4. Maegan didn't see Frederick smile _____.

Gareth continued to sleep more or less peacefully, and Arianne let her thoughts wander as she watched him and waited for night to fall. She tried not to **reproach herself** too much for what she had done. As much as she hated it, there was no escaping the fact that she was a vampire and drinking blood is what vampires do. Okay, Arianne thought, she had managed for well over a century **to feed** only **on** animal blood.

growl	Knurren
dusk	Abend-dämmerung
wicked	boshaft
to reproach oneself	sich Vorwürfe machen
to feed (on)	sich ernähren (von)

This had weakened her special abilities, but made it a bit easier for her to accept her **fate**.

At least she had had enough self-control to stop before doing any real harm to Gareth. She was fairly confident that he was going to be all right, and as long as he didn't wake up at the wrong moment, he would not remember what had happened. The hardest part was that she could not forget the sensations that had **engulfed her** in his presence. It was more, much more than the exquisite taste of his blood. She **had been consumed by** desire for this stranger even though she knew practically nothing about him. She had been convinced that such feelings had died with Rhys.

Oh no, Arianne, don't go there. You cannot let yourself think about Rhys and Jonas now. You have to **keep your wits about you** and stay focused on getting yourself and Gareth out of this cave without being seen.

Arianne pulled herself out of the past and looked outside. Yes, it was time. Darkness had finally come, and she could put her plan into action. She glanced back down at Gareth and saw that he remained in a deep slumber. Slipping his rucksack over her shoulders, she knelt down and put her arms around him. Then, as if he weighed no more than a feather, she lifted him up and began to walk out of the cave.

As soon as she reached the path outside, she began running down the mountain. Trees and rocks **whizzed by** as she increased her **pace**. She wanted to reach her car that she had left yesterday at the Visitor Centre. Avoiding the normal paths, she stopped only

fate	Schicksal
to engulf sb.	jmd. über-wältigen, verschlingen
to be con-sumed by	verzehrt werden von
to keep one's wits about one	einen kühlen Kopf bewahren
⚡ to whizz by	vorbeifliegen
pace	Tempo

occasionally to use her **heightened** senses of sight, hearing and smell to make sure that there were no people around who might **unwittingly** see the bizarre night flight. While running, she also kept her senses partially tuned to Gareth, ready to respond to the first signs of his wakening. For miles and miles, he did not move once, but just as she reached the bottom of the mountain, he began to **stir**. Arianne stopped immediately and placed him gently on the ground.

"Sir, sir, wake up, sir," she shouted and began to pat him on both cheeks.

At the sound of a woman's voice, Gareth's eyes opened. He felt completely disoriented. Where was he? What was going on? It was dark and he was lying on something hard and cold. For some reason, someone was slapping him on the face. Shaking his head, he tried to sit up, but a strong hand held him down.

"Please don't move yet," a **lilting** female voice said. "I first want to check and see if you are injured."

"And don't try and talk just yet," the voice added before Gareth could say anything. "Save your strength. I found you passed out near this path leading to the Mountain Centre, and I have no idea how long you've been unconscious."

heightened	geschärft, gesteigert
unwittingly	unbeabsichtig-terweise
to stir	sich rühren, sich bewegen
lilting	fröhlich, mit singendem Tonfall

Gareth also had no idea what had happened to him. He had vague memories of hiking, a rain storm and having had an accident. For some reason, he reached for his leg. His hiking trousers were torn and felt sticky, but the leg appeared to be uninjured. In fact, nothing was hurting, he just felt extremely tired and confused.

"Please," he murmured, "help me sit up, I think I'm fine."

Übung 7: What's wrong? Erklären Sie auf Englisch, warum die folgenden Aussagen falsch sind!

1. Feeding only on animal blood makes Arianne stronger.

   _____

2. Arianne's very worried Gareth will remember what happened in the cave.

   _____

3. Gareth was restless during the run down the mountain.

   _____

4. Gareth woke up when Arianne kissed him.

   _____

A soft hand slipped under his back and helped him sit up. Something about that hand felt familiar. The woman's voice seemed to ring a bell as well. As she pushed him into a sitting position, a name popped into Gareth's head. Arianne. But he didn't know anyone called Arianne; at least he didn't think he did.

"So, tell me, how do you feel? Do you know who you are, do you remember what happened?" Arianne asked nervously.

This was the moment when she would see if she had really been able to **wipe Gareth's memory** of the **incident** in the cave.

"I feel, well, a bit disoriented, but otherwise okay. My name is Gareth Richards and I remember everything."

His words made Arianne **gasp**.

"Everything, that is, up to the moment I started out on my hike. I think that was yesterday, or maybe the day before. After that, it's all a bit **blurry**, but I think I had some kind of accident."

"Are you by any chance the famous film star Gareth Richards?"

Arianne was relieved that her plan had indeed worked and now wanted to change the subject as quickly as possible.

"Yes, that's me. But, I promise, this is not a film set. I'm taking a break from work at the moment.

to wipe sb.'s memory	jds. Erinnerungen löschen
incident	Ereignis
to gasp	nach Luft schnappen, keuchen
blurry	verschwommen, unscharf
to giggle	kichern
pitch-dark	stockdunkel

And apparently, I am really lucky that I didn't break anything during my great escape from civilization."

Arianne **giggled** at his play on words then asked him if he thought he could stand up.

Übung 8: Translation. Lesen Sie weiter und ergänzen Sie den Text mit der Übersetzung der deutschen Begriffe!

With her assistance, Gareth slowly 1. auf die Beine kommen

_____. It was **pitch-dark**, so he

could not see his 2. Retterin _____

and briefly wondered how she had 3. schaffen

_____ to see him at all. He was 4. ablenken

_____ from that thought as he caught a

5. Hauch _____ of her scent. That, too,

6. bekannt vorkommen _____.

21

Arianne realized that it was time to move on with the next part of her plan. "If you think you can walk, Mr Richards, my car is close by. I think it might be best for you to see a doctor, just to be on the safe side."

"No, I don't think that will be necessary. I really feel fine, only a bit tired. My hotel is in Cardiff, so perhaps you could drop me at the nearest train station, and I can make my way from there."
Arianne hesitated.

Her home was just outside of Cardiff, and it would be no problem to drive him to his hotel and then take her leave. Besides, that

to neglect to do sth.	versäumen, etw. zu tun
to chide sb.	jmd. tadeln
to give sth. a light squeeze	etw. sanft drücken

way, she would have a couple of hours to make sure the memory wiping was not just a temporary thing.

As she made the spontaneous offer to take him all the way to his hotel, Gareth smiled gratefully and offered her his hand.

"I'm afraid you have the advantage over me. You know who I am, but I **neglected to** ask you your name."

When she responded with "Arianne, Arianne Gwynn," Gareth almost lost his balance. **Chiding** himself for his silliness, he told her he was pleased to make her acquaintance.

"Please, call me Gareth," he offered. "And thank you so much for your help."

As she took his hand in hers, the touch of his skin once again made Arianne shiver with pleasure. Why was it that she responded so strongly to this man, she wondered?

Gareth also felt the attraction between them. Her hand was cool, though, almost cold, as he **gave it a slight squeeze**.

Although it was extremely pleasant, the pressure was enough to bring Arianne to her senses. She pulled her hand from his and spoke a bit abruptly.

"All right, Gareth, let's get you to the car and be on our way."

The path to the car park was unlit, and Gareth wondered how Arianne could find the way. Her steps were sure and confident, though, almost as if she knew the way by heart or could see in the dark. She guided him to the space where her Range Rover with **tinted** windows was waiting.

Out of habit, Gareth made for the right side of the car before he remembered that in Great Britain, that was where the driver sat.

"Yes, I know," Arianne said, "it must be odd for you coming from the States and seeing us driving on the other side of road."

"That's one of the reasons I decided not to rent a car but use the excellent public transport system instead," Gareth explained.

"Well, **belt up** and try to enjoy the ride, Gareth. Once we get to the main road, it will take us about an hour to reach Cardiff."

Arianne started the engine and prepared to enjoy the short drive. She still got a kick out of driving. Back in **the Victorian Age** when she had been born, women had not had much freedom, and she definitely enjoyed **being her own woman**.

Gareth caught her eye and smiled. However, something was bothering him.

"Arianne, if I turn up at the hotel looking like this, someone is going to notice. The last thing I need is to see headlines in one of the **tabloids** speculating about 'Gareth's Wild Nights in Wales'. Is there any place we could stop along the way where I could clean up?"

Arianne thought it through before replying. Their route would take them almost directly past her home. The easiest thing would be to stop off there. Gareth was still showing

tinted	getönt
to belt up	sich anschnallen
the Victorian Age	das viktorianische Zeitalter (1837-1901)
to be one's own woman	eine selbstständige Frau sein
tabloid	Boulevardzeitung

no signs of remembering what had really happened in the cave, so it seemed safe enough to take the risk. Before she knew it, she heard herself inviting him for a brief visit to her cottage.

Gareth was secretly thrilled at the idea of seeing where Arianne lived and having a bit more time alone with her.

"Once again, Arianne, thank you. I don't know how I will ever be able to repay you for your kindness."

Hoping she wasn't making a huge mistake, Arianne floored the accelerator, and sped through the night.

Übung 9: Fill in the blanks. Vervollständigen Sie die Sätze mit Vokabeln aus dem Text!

1. If something is familiar it _____.

2. When there is absolutely no light it is _____.

3. If something is funny, you can laugh or _____.

4. To be safe, _____ when travelling by car.

Maegan had made up her mind at last.

She touched Frederick's arm and said, "Darling, I just want to go downstairs and have a look around. Perhaps I can find something that will tell us more about what Arianne has been up to all these years."

"All right, dearest. But be careful not to disturb anything that might arouse her suspicions," he warned.

"Of course I won't," she reassured him, even though that was exactly what she planned to do.

⚡ to floor the accelerator	Vollgas geben
to arouse sth.	etw. erwecken, erregen

2 Dawn's Flight

Arianne's car seemed to eat up the miles. At first, Gareth had asked Arianne questions about Wales and the areas they were driving through. But after an hour or so, he began to touch on more personal topics and asked her to tell him about herself.

This was not something Arianne really wanted to get into, but she didn't see how she could politely refuse to answer.

"Well, what do you want to know, Gareth?"

"The usual, I suppose. Stuff like age, occupation, **marital status**, children, hobbies and so on. Everything a man wants to know about a beautiful, mysterious woman who found him passed out in a deserted national park."

Though come to think of it, just how had she managed that, Gareth wondered.

Arianne tried to think how she could reply without giving too much away and decided to stick as closely to the truth as possible.

marital status	Familienstand
composer	Komponistin
triple harp	(walisische) Tripelharfe
to earn one's keep	seinen Lebens-unterhalt ver-dienen
score	*hier*: Filmmusik

"I'm a musician and **composer**. Perhaps you know that Wales is famous for its folk music. I play the harp and the **triple harp**, but these days, I mostly **earn my keep** composing music, mainly for the film industry. As a matter of fact, Gareth, I just finished working on a **score** for one of your films a couple of weeks ago."

"Really? That's an amazing coincidence," he exclaimed. "But I don't remember seeing your name listed as the composer for the film's music. In fact, **if memory serves**, a man created the music for it."

"Yes, that's right. I go by a different name for work purposes," she explained. "It's just, um, easier that way."

Keeping her true identity hidden was the real reason, of course, but Arianne couldn't explain that to Gareth.

"Anyway," she continued, "as to the rest of 'the Arianne story', my work keeps me fairly busy, so I don't have much time left for hobbies. I do love reading, though."

At that, she stopped talking in the hope that he would ask her more about her profession and keep away from **touchier** topics. Gareth found it odd that Arianne used a male pseudonym. Something about this woman just **didn't add up**.

Übung 10: Idiomatic expressions. Schreiben Sie die Sätze mit Wendungen aus dem obigen Abschnitt neu!

1. For professional reasons , Arianne uses a pseudonym.

_____

2. Arianne decided to be honest .

_____

3. She makes her living as a composer.

_____

4. Gareth is pretty sure that a man composed the film's score.

_____

if memory serves	wenn ich mich recht erinnere
touchy	heikel, empfindlich
to not add up	keinen Sinn ergeben
tentatively	zögernd
to overwhelm sb.	jmd. überwältigen
in earnest	richtig, ernsthaft

"But, Arianne," Gareth asked, "you must have a personal life? I mean, it really is none of my business, but I'm curious to learn more about you. You interest me."

With his last comment, Gareth tentatively reached over and touched the hand that was closest to him.

The feel of his hand on hers was exciting and oddly reassuring. Arianne decided to trust him with part of the truth.

"I am 28 years old, Gareth, but I feel a lot older. You see, I was married and had a child, a son."

Her voice lowered to almost a whisper, she continued, "But they were both killed a long time ago in a tragic accident at sea."

Arianne's eyes began to blur with tears, as even after all these years the memories threatened to overwhelm her.

Gareth wanted more than anything else to comfort her. He didn't know what to say, though, and instead of speaking, he moved his hand to her face and brushed away a tear.

Arianne shook her head. "Please, Gareth, don't. Don't be nice to me. I don't deserve it and it just makes it harder for me."

At that, the tears she was trying so hard to contain suddenly began flowing in earnest.

Gareth wasn't sure if he understood what she meant, but removed his hand.

"Arianne, maybe you should pull over for a few minutes and take a moment to collect yourself," he suggested quietly.

Arianne didn't want to stop, but she knew it was foolish to keep driving with her eyes almost blinded by tears. She spotted a petrol station just ahead and a few seconds later, halted the car.

"I'm sorry, Gareth. I don't know what came over me. Just give me a second and we can be back on our way."

"Take all the time you need, Arianne. It must have been so awful, losing your family like that," he said gently. "Do you want to talk about it?"

to be on the verge of sth.	am Rande von etw. stehen
to anticipate sth.	etw. erwarten
to faint	in Ohnmacht fallen

"No, definitely not. Talking won't bring Rhys and Jonas back to me, and as I said, it happened a long time ago. I should be over it by now, but sometimes the memories come, and it hurts as if I just lost them all over again."

Gareth sensed that Arianne **was on the verge of** breaking down into tears again. "Then we won't talk," he agreed.

Unbuckling his seatbelt, he reached for her and gathered her into his strong arms. He'd been wondering what it would be like to hold her almost from the first moment back in the park. Now he knew. She was soft, so incredibly soft, yet at the same time he felt her hidden strength. What surprised him was how cool her body felt beneath the cloak she was wearing.

For the second time in less than 24 hours, Arianne gave in to temptation. She melted into Gareth's embrace and delighted in the feel of his arms around her. She felt his finger slowly lifting her chin and parted her lips slightly, **anticipating** his kiss. As their lips met, she thought she might **faint** at the sensation. It was better, so much better than she had imagined. She returned his kiss with all the buried passion inside her.

Astonished at her response, Gareth deepened the kiss. He wanted more, so much more and pulled her even closer.

For a moment, Arianne thought about just letting her body take over. But she knew it would be a mistake. She just couldn't let Gareth get too close. It would be dangerous for them both.

"Gareth, we have to stop," she gasped and tried to end the embrace. "We're both far too old to be **snogging** in a car."

"Snogging, what's that? Oh, of course, British English again.

⚡ to snog (GB)	(rum)knutschen
⚡ to make out (US)	(rum)knutschen, rummachen
the rat race	ständiger Konkurrenzkampf

You mean **making out**, kissing, that sort of thing," Gareth grinned. "Well, I am not going to apologize, my lady. If you don't want to, um, snog in the car, let's find a place that's more suited to continuing where we left off."

Arianne laughed, something else that she rarely did. In addition to the physical attraction between them, Gareth seemed to be able to make her feel almost happy.

"Okay, sir. No promises about the kissing part, but I'll get us back on the road."

Übung 11: Tenses. Lesen Sie weiter und unterstreichen Sie die richtige Variante!

They 1. spent / were spending the rest of the drive 2. get / getting to know each other a bit better. Gareth 3. was explaining / explained that he 4. has come / had come to Wales because he 5. needs / needed a break from **the rat race** in Hollywood.

6. "I've always wanted / "I always wanted to visit the place my family came from, but never seemed to find time. For the past years, 7. it's been / it was one film after the other."

29

Now it was Arianne's turn to let curiosity get the better of her. "And what about time for romance, Gareth? I don't remember ever hearing[i] that you were married, but there must be millions of women out there dying for a chance to go out with you."

Nach **to remember** in der Bedeutung „sich erinnern" folgt immer das Gerundium (ing-Form).
I don't remember ever hearing ... bedeutet also:
Ich kann mich nicht daran erinnern, jemals gehört zu haben ...

"Well, I have had a few relationships, but I don't know, somehow I never had that 'fireworks going off, butterflies in my stomach, bells ringing' sort of feeling."

Abruptly, Gareth stopped talking. He had experienced exactly that feeling – with Arianne! He suddenly felt warm at the very thought of the kisses and caresses they had shared.

"Arianne, would it be okay if I let down the window? I could do with a bit of fresh air."

Arianne nodded in agreement and, even though she had no use for air and oxygen, enjoyed the feel of the breeze on her skin.

They reached the outskirts of Cardiff just before 10:00 p.m., and Arianne left the motorway and turned off onto the road leading to Pentyrch Village. Out of habit, she kept looking in the rear-view mirror to make sure she was not being followed. After several more turns, she finally slowed the car in front of her cottage

oxygen	Sauerstoff
outskirts *pl*	Stadtrand

that stood alone on a dimly lit street. Just as she began to turn into the drive and park, her eyes widened. There in the front sitting room the curtains were slightly parted.

"No, it can't be," Arianne exclaimed, and immediately threw the car into reverse.

At that moment, Gareth saw the front door to her home fly open. A dark shape with outstretched arms seemed to jump out of it and began moving towards them at an incredible speed. The figure was that of a man, and he was staring directly at Gareth with, no, it was impossible, silver eyes. He shouted something,

to screech	quietschen
to drown out sth.	etw. übertönen
frantically	verzweifelt, hektisch
stunned	fassungslos
agitation	Aufregung
to blaze	(auf)lodern, glühen

but the tyres screeched on the asphalt and drowned out his words.

"Gareth, close the window. Now!"

Arianne yanked the steering wheel to the right and got the car headed back towards Cardiff. She looked about frantically, trying to see if anyone was following them.

Stunned, Gareth hit the button to shut the window.

"Arianne, what's happening? Who was that? And where are we going?" he asked, trying to make sense of what he had just seen. He had no idea what was going on.

"Gareth, please be quiet. I have to think. You'll just have to trust me for a second."

In her agitation, Arianne forgot about what happened to her when she was upset.

"Arianne, you… your eyes…," he whispered.

And as he saw that they were now blazing just as silver as those of the frightening figure at her house, Gareth began to shake. Then he noticed Arianne's teeth, no, not teeth, they had become longer and more pointed. As the word "fangs" popped into his confused brain, Gareth suddenly knew he had seen them before.

The entire scene in the cave came flooding back into his mind. He shook his head in denial. It just was not possible.

1. Where is Arianne's cottage located?

   _____

2. Why does Gareth want to let down the window?

   _____

3. What makes Arianne rush away from her cottage?

   _____

4. What makes Gareth realize that Arianne is a vampire?

   _____

As the car raced towards the motorway, Gareth's only thought was that he had to escape. He **lunged towards** the passenger door. But Arianne had anticipated his move and grabbed his arm. Her grip was so firm that it was impossible to move.

"Gareth, please, I can explain. You can't jump out of the car now, you'll be killed."

"I'd rather die trying to get away than be killed by a… by a… whatever you are," he shouted.

"Vampire. That's the word you are looking for. And yes, that's what I am," Arianne replied calmly.

Still keeping her hold on Gareth, Arianne **accelerated**.

to lunge towards	sich stürzen auf
to accelerate	beschleunigen

"Gareth," she continued in a low, calm tone, "you have no reason to be afraid of me. I would never, ever harm you."

Gareth couldn't believe his ears. "Not harm me? You already did, Arianne. You didn't find me on that path. You were in the cave and you, you..."

pursuit	Verfolgung
⚡ to fall into sb.'s clutches	jmd. in die Hände fallen
as the saying goes	wie es so schön heißt

His mouth refused to say the words out loud. The same lips that had kissed him so passionately had actually drunk his blood. The thought should have been disgusting. But Gareth was surprised to discover that his trembling was not only caused by fear.

"So. You remember. That sometimes happens, and I'm sorry, Gareth, really sorry. If you like, I can try and wipe your memory again, and you will forget all about this – and me. But I can't do it now. I have to get us both to safety. Frederick saw the car and I'm pretty sure he saw you as well."

"Frederick? Is that the… the 'thing' that came after us?" Gareth still couldn't say the word vampire.

"Yes. Frederick Wellen, and I suspect he's not alone. He and his mate Maegan have been searching for me for, well, you don't really want to know how long. Now that he's found me, he won't give up the pursuit easily, and I imagine he – or they – are close on our heels."

Gareth took a deep breath and tried to steady his nerves. "So my options are either to stick with you, or fall into the clutches of the evil couple Frederick and Maegan?"

For some reason, he felt almost able to try and make a joke.

"Well, Gareth, as the saying almost goes, 'better the vampire you know than the ones that you don't.' "

Gareth thought about that and decided that if Arianne had wanted to kill him, she could have done it back in the cave. One thing was for sure, though. As soon as they got to wherever it was they were heading, she had a hell of a lot of explaining to do.

Übung 13: If-clauses. Bringen Sie die Wörter in die richtige Reihenfolge, um if-Sätze zu bilden!

1. jumps | killed | he | out | car | Gareth | the | be | of | might | if

   _____

2. the | Arianne | in | done | had | if | wanted | she | cave | to | could | it | kill | Gareth | have

   _____

   _____

3. curtains | the | if | opened | have | warning | would | the | Maegan | no | had | Arianne | hadn't

   _____

   _____

4. try | will | her | Frederick | kill | to | Arianne | he | finds | if

   _____

"Maegan, come here," Frederick shouted, furious that Arianne had somehow managed to escape.

In his rage, he struck the doorframe with his bare hand, splintering the wood. He had been so incredibly close to catching her and wondered what – or who – had made Arianne suspect that something was wrong. As Maegan obeyed his call and appeared behind him, Frederick spun around and gripped her upper arms.

Shaking her violently, he demanded, "Tell me how she knew; tell me what **tipped her off**."

Maegan **whimpered** in pain at his cruel grip. "I don't know, Frederick, really I don't. Perhaps our scent **gave us away**."

to tip sb. off	jmd. einen Hinweis geben
to whimper	wimmern
to give sb. away	jmd. verraten
white lie	Notlüge
donor	(Blut-)Spender

"I doubt that is the reason," Frederick spat. "Arianne was never a powerful vampire and as she only feeds on animals, her senses must be weakened. You must have done something that warned her!"

"Oh Frederick, I would never betray you in such a way."

Übung 14: Fill in the blanks. Lesen Sie weiter und vervollständigen Sie den Text!

It was a **white lie** and Meagan quickly **1.** c_____ up with what she hoped was a more **2.** p_____ explanation. "Well, Frederick, you haven't seen Arianne in what, over a hundred and thirty years? **3.** P_____ she has changed," she suggested.

"I **4.** s_____ it could be, and wait a **5.** m_____, there was a man with her, a human. If she is using him as a **donor**, it might **6.** b_____ that he has given her new strength."

This idea was not pleasing at all. Frederick had expected a quick and easy battle with Arianne. If she were now feeding on human blood, his task would be all the more difficult. But first, he had to find her again.

⚡ to snoop (around)	(herum-) schnüffeln
blatantly	offensichtlich, unverfroren
estate agency	Maklerbüro
to plead with sb.	jmd. anflehen
⚡ to let on that…	verraten, dass …
to abandon sth.	etw. aufgeben

"Maegan, what did you find while you were **snooping around** the house? Did you discover any clue, anything at all about where Arianne might have gone?"

Maegan knew that she had to be very careful. If Frederick caught her **blatantly** lying, he might actually turn on her.

"Well, there was one thing," she admitted. "I found her address book in a desk drawer. There were a couple of entries for businesses on Anglesey Island. One of them was a housekeeping service and another was for an **estate agency**."

Frederick's hot anger began to cool and his wicked smile reappeared. "Well done, my love, well done. Now why, I wonder, would our Arianne need to have contact with such services? Could it be she has property on the island? Well, it's certainly worth investigating. But, Maegan, I think it would be best if I went on my own. I'm beginning to suspect that you might have a conflict of interests, or are you feeling a bit guilty?"

Maegan denied this and **pleaded with** Frederick to let her come along on the hunt for Arianne. She could not stand it when he was displeased with her. Nor could she **let on that** she had parted the curtains as a signal to Arianne, or that she wished Frederick would **abandon** his plan.

"But, darling, how will you manage on your own? If you are right, and Arianne is stronger now, you'll need help."

"Oh, who said anything about **going it alone**, Maegan? Arianne has broken the first rule of vampire safety. She is travelling with a human. I think our friends the Midnight Hunters would be very interested in that bit of information. And you, my dear, are going to leave for London right now and get in touch with their leader Rory. Tell him to please send a couple of his strongest vampires to Anglesey Island. By the time they arrive, I should have found Arianne, and if they're lucky, I might let them in on the kill."

to go it alone	etw. im Allein-gang machen
vicious	bösartig, grausam
to foil sb.'s plans	jds. Pläne vereiteln
sinister	finster, unheilvoll
to rummage	(durch)wühlen

Maegan shuddered at the thought of Rory and his gang. They were the most cruel and **vicious** vampires of all. She could not disobey Frederick, but perhaps there was a way to **foil his plans** without him knowing it, she thought as she nodded in agreement.

"As you wish, Frederick."

Avoiding his eyes, she touched his shoulder in a gesture of fare-well.

With a **sinister** laugh, Frederick watched as she disappeared into the night before he, too, vanished.

Arianne let herself relax slightly as she parked the car in a garage near Cardiff airport. She had rented it ages ago as part of her many back-up plans in case Frederick ever found her. Gareth looked at her enquiringly as she opened the door and got out of the car.

"Come on, Gareth, we have to move fast."

Arianne walked rapidly past a second car and over to a wardrobe at the front of the garage. She pulled open its mirrored door and began **rummaging** inside.

"Here, take these and put them on," she told him.

1. Maegan found Arianne's address book in a drawer.

_____

2. Arianne has broken the first rule of vampire safety.

_____

3. He should send a couple of his strongest vampires to Anglesey Island.

_____

_____

4. I might let them in on the kill.

_____

Gareth caught the items she had just thrown him: a pair of fresh trousers, a white shirt, a simple jacket with matching leather shoes.

Looking up, he glimpsed Arianne pulling off her cloak and underlying skirt and blouse. The sight of her in nothing but the scantiest of bras and knickers made him forget for a moment that he was on the run with a vampire. Arianne didn't give him much time to enjoy the view, though. She slipped a dark-blue silk dress over her head and pulled on a pair of ballerinas.

"Gareth, get changed," she snapped. "We have no time to lose."

Turning around, Gareth also disrobed and tried on the new clothes. Everything fit perfectly, and he wondered how Arianne just happened to have a complete set of men's clothing in his size. But okay, much stranger things had happened in the past few hours.

He opened his mouth to ask a question, but Arianne cut him off.

Übung 16: Choose the correct alternative. Lesen Sie weiter und markieren Sie die richtige Variante!

"So Gareth, here's the **1.** message / plan . You have a choice to make. I can do as I told you and try and **2.** hide / clear your memory again of all that has happened. Then you can **3.** get on / ride a plane back to California and return to your life in real films. The other **4.** option / conclusion is that you decide to trust me completely, **5.** here and now / now and forever . If you do, we'll leave here together and make our **6.** path / way to Anglesey Island."

At the sound of that name, Gareth drew in his breath and let it out in a soft whistle.

Arianne ignored him and carried on with her rushed speech. "I have a house there where I think we can hide out for a few days. It's been a while since I visited it, but I think it will suit our needs. When we arrive, I promise to explain everything and do my best to answer all your questions. Most of all, I promise to do all that's possible to **keep you out of harm's way**."

scanty	knapp
to disrobe	sich entkleiden
to keep sb. out of harm's way	jmd. vor Schaden bewahren

Arianne ended her ultimatum and waited to see how Gareth would respond.

to brace oneself for	sich gefasst machen auf

Gareth knew he had to decide immediately. I really must be insane, he thought to himself. No one in their right mind would even hesitate for a second to get away from a vampire, no matter how beautiful or sexy she was. Gareth struggled between what he knew to be the safe choice and the more dangerous, but strangely thrilling, one. It was not just because of Arianne that he was tempted, very tempted, to stay. There was only one thing to do to help him make the best choice.

Slowly, he walked over to Arianne and took her hands. Bending his head to hers, he placed his lips on her lovely hair in a gentle kiss.

To Arianne it seemed like a goodbye gesture, and she braced herself for his words of departure. They did not come. Instead, Gareth let go of her hands and pulled her into his arms. It was like coming home, and for a few seconds, they stood in the silent embrace, just holding each other.

Übung 17: Synonyms. Suchen Sie im Text die Entsprechungen zu den folgenden Verben!

1. inhale _____

2. release _____

3. keep safe _____

4. continue _____

5. prepare _____

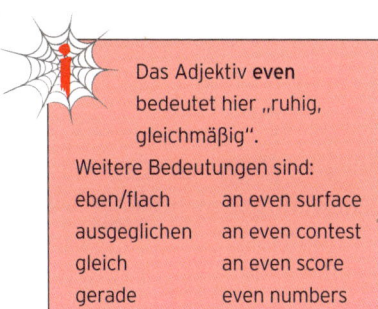

Das Adjektiv **even** bedeutet hier „ruhig, gleichmäßig".

Weitere Bedeutungen sind:

eben/flach	an even surface
ausgeglichen	an even contest
gleich	an even score
gerade	even numbers

"I'm going with you, Arianne," Gareth said softly. "I don't know why, but I don't want to be without you. It may be the most foolish thing I've ever done, but come on. Let's go. Um, by the way, are we taking a plane to the island?"

"No, we'll take my spare car, the **all-terrain vehicle** here. I don't think we should wait for the first flight tomorrow morning. It's also much better for me if we travel by night as sunlight is not the healthiest thing for vampires."

Arianne examined Gareth's expression closely to see how he would react to her use of the "V" word. She saw his eyes widen slightly and that he was taking deep, even breaths to try and calm his instinctive fear.

"There's still time to change your mind, Gareth," she assured him.

"No," Gareth replied and squared his shoulders. "I'm ready when you are, Arianne. Let's hit the road."

Maegan arrived by train in London just after 2:00 a.m.

Well, it's the right time of night for tracking down the Midnight Hunters, she thought.

She had no desire to visit their **hang-outs**, but knew that if she didn't do exactly what Frederick wanted, his anger would **know no bounds**.

She made her way from Paddington Station to a nearby club. Going through the entrance took all her courage. Rory and his gang were unpre-

all-terrain vehicle (ATV)	Geländewagen
⚡ **hang-out**	Treff, Stammlokal
to know no bounds	keine Grenzen kennen

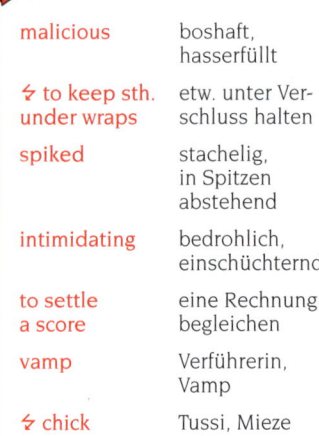

malicious	boshaft, hasserfüllt
⚡ to keep sth. under wraps	etw. unter Verschluss halten
spiked	stachelig, in Spitzen abstehend
intimidating	bedrohlich, einschüchternd
to settle a score	eine Rechnung begleichen
vamp	Verführerin, Vamp
⚡ chick	Tussi, Mieze

dictable, and her success depended on whether they were fed and satisfied, or getting ready to go hunting.

"Well, well, well, what have we here?" a deep, **malicious** voice cut into her thoughts.

"It looks as if Frederick's little woman is out on her own," another voice, also male, replied.

"Hello, Rory," Maegan smiled as she addressed him. "How wonderful to see you again after all this time. I hope you and your family are well," she added politely in an effort to hide her anxiety.

"What's it to you, Maegan? I thought Frederick **kept** you tightly **under wraps**. Whatever brings you from your sleepy old Wales to our territory in the big city?"

With that Rory got up from the sofa he had been sitting on. He was huge, and his **spiked** hairstyle made him seem even more **intimidating**.

Maegan decided to cut the small talk and get her task over with as quickly as possible.

"Frederick sent me. He's found Arianne at last and he needs your help."

Rory almost exploded with laughter. "Hey guys, did you hear that? Our old friend Freddy thinks he can send his girlfriend in here on a mission, and we will all just be ready and willing to help him **settle his score**."

The rest of the vampire gang, who were scattered about the room, joined in his laughter.

Übung 18: Translation. Lesen Sie weiter und übersetzen Sie Maegans Monolog ins Deutsche!

"It's not funny," Maegan interrupted. "It seems that Arianne has not only finally turned up, she has a human with her. A man. Frederick is certain that she's using this guy as a donor and has most likely told him all about being a vampire and our world. You all know the punishment for that! I don't think it's anything to laugh about."

_____

_____

_____

_____

_____

_____

_____

In one fluid move, Rory leapt up and slapped Maegan hard. "Listen, you vampire **vamp**, no one, no one at all comes in here and tells me and my boys what to do. If your Frederick can't manage one weak vampire **chick** on his own, he deserves what he gets. Things are hot enough for us here in London at the

⚡ to tell sb. where to get off	jmd. was husten, jmd. ordentlich Bescheid sagen
to provoke sb.	jmd. provozieren
⚡ in the nick of time	gerade noch rechtzeitig
⚡ to hatch a plan	einen Plan aushecken

moment, and I'm not getting involved in Frederick's little love-story-gone-bad revenge deal. Everybody knows that he has never got over Arianne leaving him. Now get out of here and tell him from me to do his own dirty work."

Maegan was dying **to tell Rory where to get off**. She thought better of it, though. Her idea had gone exactly according to plan. There was no reason to **provoke** Rory or one of the others.

"All right, Rory, please calm down. I didn't mean to upset you or try and order you around, it's just..."

As Rory raised his hand to hit her again, Maegan jumped back just **in the nick of time**. Turning so he could not see her smile of satisfaction, she made a flying leap and was back on the London streets.

What she failed to see was that she was no longer alone. Rory and one of his gang members had followed her out and were busy **hatching a plan** of their own.

3 Dawn's Delight

The ATV seemed to eat up the miles. At this hour, there was very little traffic on the roads. Arianne had decided not to take the most direct route to Anglesey. That would have meant going back in the direction where Frederick and Maegan were still likely to be. Instead, they had headed west on the M4 towards Swansea.

When they stopped to fill up the car, Gareth took the opportunity to buy a sandwich and a cup of coffee. He couldn't remember when he had last eaten and was starving. He settled back into his seat as Arianne turned the car north and continued their journey right across Wales.

"Arianne, how often do you need to… ah, well… eat – or should I say drink?" he asked while adding sugar to his coffee.

"It varies, but about once a week seems to be enough for me. If I feed less often, I become quite weak."

Arianne glanced towards him as he took another bite of his sandwich. "Does it bother you much to think about me feeding, Gareth, especially the fact that my last meal was, well, you?"

The question made Gareth feel a bit **queasy**, and he put the rest of his

queasy	mulmig, übel

sandwich aside. At the moment, he really did not want to think about what had happened in the cave, or what would happen if Arianne suddenly got hungry again.

Übung 19: Fill in the blanks. Lesen Sie weiter und ergänzen Sie die fehlenden Wörter!

"So, tell me, where **1.** e _____ are we running off to?" Gareth asked.

His sudden change of **2.** s _____ told Arianne that even though Gareth was **3.** c _____ about her vampire existence, he wasn't quite **4.** r _____ for all the details. She decided to **5.** g _____ him time.

"Well, Holy Island is an island off the larger Isle of Anglesey, the north-western tip of Wales. The population is around..."

Gareth interrupted her. "Arianne, I don't want a geography lesson, I want to know about our hideaway!"

"Funny," she murmured, "that's what Rhys called it. He gave the house to me as an engagement present and said it would be our 'secret place' where we would always have time just for us. It was our 'love nest' and we had some of the most wonderful moments in our marriage there." Arianne's voice grew softer at the memories.

Seeing that Arianne was getting emotional again, Gareth asked her where exactly the house was.

"It's just outside a village called Rhoscolyn, in the southern part of the island. The house faces the sea and it's just a short walk down to the beach. I think we will be safe there."

Gareth hoped so. "Are you worried that Frederick and Maegan

to murmur	murmeln
engagement	*hier*: Verlobung

might have **picked up on our trail**? Do they know about the house?"

Arianne considered her answer carefully. "I don't think so, but I can't be certain. I've known Maegan all my life. You see, she and Rhys were brother and sister, and they lived next door

to pick up on sb.'s trail	auf jds. Spur stoßen
to confide sth. in sb.	jmd. etw. anvertrauen
⚡ **to be on the creepy side**	ein wenig unheimlich sein
inappropriate advances *pl*	unangemessene Annäherungsversuche

to me and my family. Maegan was my closest friend, even before she became my sister-in-law. I **confided** almost everything **in her**, but I never told her about the house. I couldn't help sharing with her that Rhys had given me a very special present, though. And of course she noticed that after our marriage, we were often gone for days at a time."

"Well, that sounds as if at least Maegan can't be in the picture," Gareth replied. "What about Frederick?"

Arianne explained that Frederick had been one of Rhys's business associates in his family-owned ⓘ shipping company. "Frederick was involved in importing and exporting all sorts of goods. I always thought he **was on the creepy side**, but he fascinated Maegan and she wanted nothing more than to be his wife. At the time, Frederick didn't seem to be interested in her, though, and was always, well, making **inappropriate advances** towards me.

Steht ein zusammengesetztes Adjektiv als Attribut vor einem Substantiv, so werden die Einzelbegriffe im britischen Englisch im Normalfall mit einem Bindestrich verbunden.

Maegan saw him trying to kiss me once and became extremely jealous. That's one of the things that destroyed our friendship."

"Was Frederick... I mean, is he in love with you?" The very thought of Frederick touching Arianne made Gareth's stomach turn.

1. "Arianne, I want to know about our hideaway!" Gareth said.

   _____

2. "It's just outside a village called Rhoscolyn," Arianne told him.

   _____

3. "I don't think so, but I can't be certain," she said.

   _____

4. "Well, that sounds as if Maegan can't be in the picture," he replied.

   _____

"Frederick doesn't know what love is," Arianne replied after a long moment. "I don't think he has ever experienced that emotion, even as a human."

"And how did he become a, a...," Gareth finally said it, "vampire?"

Arianne didn't know. Frederick had never talked about it. She only knew he was a much older vampire and that he had been born in London.

"Gareth, I don't know much about Frederick's history before he was turned."

"Turned? Is that what you call it?"

To his surprise, Gareth noticed that it was getting a bit easier to talk about such things, and he found himself reaching once more for his sandwich.

"Yes. That's what it's called when a vampire uses either force or seduction to **drain** a human of all their blood. If the human then drinks the vampire's blood, they are 'turned', meaning they become a vampire, too."

"And if the human doesn't?" Gareth asked.

Arianne took her eyes away from the road and met his eyes. "Then the person dies."

to drain sb.	*hier*: jmd. aussaugen
to probe	(nach)forschen
to no avail	vergeblich

For a few moments, neither of them spoke. Arianne turned her attention back to driving, and Gareth took a moment to pluck up the courage to **probe** further.

"And you, Arianne, how were you turned?"

The pain in her voice as she replied was shattering. "Frederick did it. And then he killed Rhys and Jonas."

Frederick drummed his fingers impatiently on the darkened window of his sports car. He had driven directly from Arianne's cottage to the Britannia Bridge and crossed over the Menai Strait to Anglesey Island. Along the way, he had constantly been on the lookout for some sign of Arianne and her male companion, but **to no avail**. He had also had no luck reaching Maegan on her mobile.

He wasn't really worried but could feel himself getting angry again. Then, just as he was reaching for his phone to call her once more, it started to ring. Seeing Maegan's name on the display, he yelled, "What the hell took you so long?"

"Now, Frederick, is that any way to speak to an old friend?" a male voice reproached him.

"Who's there?" Frederick asked in surprise.

"Don't you recognize my voice, Freddie? How very disappointing. After all, you were the one who wanted to speak with me. At least that's what your sweet messenger told me when she turned up in London."

"Rory. How kind of you to get back to me. But why are you using Maegan's phone? And speaking of Maegan, where is she and why hasn't she returned my calls?" Frederick deliberately spoke in a calm, almost uninterested tone.

Übung 21: Synonyms. Lesen Sie weiter und unterstreichen Sie die Synonyme der angegebenen Begriffe!

busy   silliness   worried   speak louder   to plan

"Oh, you needn't be concerned about Maegan. Let's just say she's, um, tied up right now and can't come to the phone. And since she doesn't need it at the moment, I borrowed it to give you a ring **for old times' sake**.

Frederick had no idea what Rory was up to and really didn't have any patience with such childish games. Raising his voice slightly, he demanded to know what Rory had done with Maegan.

"Oh, all right, Frederick, if you can't stand the **suspense**, I'll tell you. I had told her that we weren't going to help you with your dirty little plan to kill Arianne. I thought better of it, though, because, after all, one vampire deciding to **do in** another concerns us all. I want to make sure you don't cause any unwanted attention."

"You're a fine one to speak of unwanted attention, Rory. What you and the other Midnight Hunters have been up to in London lately has the entire vampire world talking," Frederick countered.

for old times' sake	um der alten Zeiten willen
suspense	Spannung
⚡ to do sb. in	jmd. kaltmachen
to counter	entgegnen, kontern
⚡ to drop a bombshell	eine Bombe platzen lassen
condescending	herablassend
to snicker	spöttisch lachen

Rory angrily told Frederick to shut up and then he dropped his bombshell. He'd taken Meagan back to the club and used what Rory called "gentle persuasion" to find out where Frederick suspected Arianne was going.

"I've sent two of the Midnight Hunters to Anglesey Island," Rory informed Frederick. "You can meet Matt and Gavin at dusk by the Four Mile Bridge near Holyhead. But you should know, Frederick, I've told them this is your fight and they are to keep a low profile. They're only supposed to give you a hand if you really need it and then report back to me."

Frederick was furious at Rory. How dare he kidnap Maegan and, even worse, how dare he speak to him in such a condescending tone?

"Fine, Rory," he said sarcastically. "I suspect I'll be able to manage without their assistance, but I'll be glad of the company. Now, would you please let me speak to Maegan?"

"No, Frederick. As soon as Matt and Gavin tell me that all is well, I'll let Maegan rush back home to your loving arms," he snickered.

Frederick wished he could reach through the phone and grab Rory around the neck, but he forced himself to remain calm.

"Well, Rory, make sure she comes back to me unharmed. I would hate to have to come all the way to London and fight you."

"Don't make empty threats, Frederick. I could tear you apart with my bare hands," Rory warned and ended the call abruptly.

Frederick shook his head to clear his thoughts. He had more urgent matters to attend to than Rory's **snide remarks**. The sun would be coming up soon. Before meeting the London vampires, he needed to do some research and find out exactly where Arianne's hiding place was. So far, he still didn't know for sure if he was on the right track.

A long-ago conversation with Rhys was **niggling at** the back of his mind. Holy Island had come up, something to do with the shipping routes to Ireland. Rhys had called the island 'my favourite place on earth' and laughingly said it held his 'dawn's delight'. At the time, Frederick had thought Rhys meant a woman, but remembering how Rhys had practically **worshipped** Arianne, he started to put two and two together. Could "dawn's delight" actually be a place?

snide remark	abfällige Bemerkung
to niggle at	nagen an, beunruhigen
to worship	anbeten
to haunt sb.	jmd. heimsuchen, verfolgen

His gaze fell on Maegan's laptop that she'd left in the car.

"Ah, the joys of modern telecommunications," he purred.

All he had to do was drive towards Holyhead and find a nice quiet place where he could spend the day. The wireless connection on the notebook would take care of the rest.

As they rounded the last bend in the road leading to her house, Arianne's thoughts were racing in circles. All the other times she had arrived here seemed to rise up and **haunt her**. She had come to Dawn's Delight as a new bride, again as a young mother and then, that horrible time, as a newly turned vampire. Then as well as now, she'd been running from Frederick. But this time, Gareth was at her side.

"Welcome, Gareth. Welcome to Dawn's Delight."

Gareth couldn't believe his ears. "Did you say 'Dawn's Delight'?"

"Yes, that's the name of the house. Didn't I mention it?"

"No, no, you never used its name. Arianne, I think it's time for me to tell you a story of my own," he said with a grin. "I just happen to know a thing or two about your **haven**."

Gareth's voice was filled with excitement as the two-story **manor house** appeared in the first **rays** of the new day. "Oh my, it's gorgeous, exactly the way my great-great grandmother described it in her diary."

"Your great-great grandmother," Arianne repeated slowly.

"Yes. Her name was Caitlin Hennessey, and in a way, Arianne, this is also my ancestral home."

Gareth turned to place an arm around her but stopped when he saw her **pensive** expression.

"Arianne, is everything okay? You're so quiet."

Arianne was in shock. Was Gareth related to Caitlin?

"I'm just astonished, that's all," she said, and shook her head. "And I can hardly wait to hear the rest. But first, let's get the car into the old stables and me out of the sun."

haven	Zufluchtsort
manor house	Landsitz, Herrenhaus
ray	Strahl
pensive	nachdenklich
upkeep	Instandhaltung
disguise	Verkleidung

Everything at Dawn's Delight was in excellent shape. Even though Arianne rarely spent time here, she had developed a system for its **upkeep**: Every 15 to 20 years, she "sold" the house to a different person who was actually herself using some **disguise**. She let an agent handle most of the details.

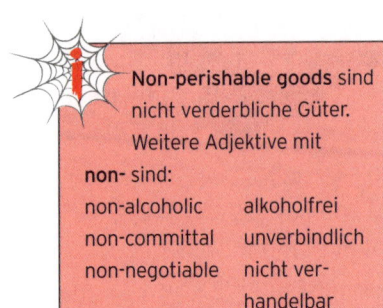

Non-perishable goods sind nicht verderbliche Güter.
Weitere Adjektive mit **non-** sind:

non-alcoholic	alkoholfrei
non-committal	unverbindlich
non-negotiable	nicht verhandelbar

The agent arranged for the house to be regularly modernized and made sure that the house and grounds were kept in order. So the house was always ready in case she decided to **pop in** at short notice. She even had the **pantry** stocked with non-perishable goods.

"Here we are, Gareth. This is the kitchen where Caitlin used to prepare such delicious meals for us."

Gareth looked around and tried to imagine what it must have been like here way back then. Arianne interrupted his daydreaming by placing a steaming mug of tea into his hand.

"Here, Gareth, sit down and drink this. I just want to check that all the curtains are drawn and that the alarm system is working before I join you."

Gareth wondered if by joining him Arianne meant she was also going to have something to drink, but quickly shook off the **eerie** thought. When she re-entered the kitchen a few minutes later, he had himself back under control.

"I should have made the connection sooner," he told her with a **wry** laugh. "Caitlin's description of you, her 'Lady Arianne', was perfect. But your reason for sending her and her husband Owen away remained a life-long mystery to her."

"I had no choice but to fire your great-great grandparents, Gareth," she tried to explain. "The last time I saw Caitlin and Owen, I was a

⚡ to pop in	vorbeischauen
pantry	Vorratskammer
eerie	unheimlich, gespenstisch
wry	trocken, ironisch
to be in mourning	trauern
⚡ to catch on (to sth.)	etw. kapieren

newly turned vampire. I had managed to escape from Frederick and needed a place to hide and adjust to what had happened."

"But, Arianne, they could have helped you. You **were in mourning** and needed friends."

Gareth still hadn't **caught on**.

"Gareth, vampires don't have friends! If I hadn't let them go, you wouldn't be here."

Übung 22: Verb forms. Lesen Sie weiter und ergänzen Sie die richtige Verbform!

"Newborn vampires **1. be** _____ especially

dangerous and **2. have** _____ almost no self-

control. As much as I cared for Caitlin and Owen, it

3. be _____ all I could do **4. keep** _____

myself from feeding on them both. If they had stayed,

I **5. do** _____ it. And what's more, Caitlin

would sooner or later have noticed that I **6. suffer**

_____ from more than the loss of my hus-

band and child."

Arianne glared at Gareth. "As you may have noticed, I don't always look the way I do right now. I'm still dangerous, Gareth." Gareth's fear rose again as he remembered the sight of her pearly teeth extending into fangs and her deep blue eyes glowing silver. It had terrified him, but he ignored the fear, thinking instead about how she had kept herself under control.

"So, that's why you gave my great-great grandparents such a generous **settlement**, but only under the condition that they use the money to immigrate to the United States."

Gareth finally understood what Arianne had done to protect his relatives and not harm them. Despite the reminder of what she was, he once again found his hand moving to cover hers. "Arianne, I guess I do have you to thank for my even being born. Caitlin and Owen were happy in their new home, but they never forgot you or Dawn's Delight." The coincidence was **mind-boggling**. His great-great grandparents had worked in this house. They had taken care of Arianne and her family. And now, here he was in that same house holding hands with her.

settlement	*hier*: Abfindung
⚡ mind-boggling	irre, verrückt
intertwined	(miteinander) verflochten
to fume	*hier*: vor Wut kochen
⚡ pal	Kumpel
to turn the tables	den Spieß umdrehen

"It seems as if our destinies really are **intertwined**," he added.

Shortly after daybreak in London, Maegan was ready to explode. She was still chained to a bed in Rory's back room at the club and had been **fuming** ever since he and his **pal** had overpowered her at the tube station. Mostly she was furious with herself for not putting up a better fight. Even worse, she had not been able to hold up against what Rory called "persuasive tactics". In the end, she had told him what he wanted to know. So she had to get out of here and somehow warn Frederick. The vampires Rory had sent to supposedly help were in fact planning to **turn the tables** and make sure that both Arianne and Frederick died.

Maegan didn't know why there was such "bad blood" between Frederick and Rory. But she had heard enough to know that

Rory hated her mate and was wickedly thrilled at the prospect of making it look as if Arianne had killed him.

The thick chains around Meagan's wrists were fastened to a metal loop on the wall behind the bed. She hadn't really tried to free herself yet because she knew Rory was still in the next room and she was afraid he would hear her. Her only chance of escape would be to completely surprise him. She couldn't wait any longer, though.

Pressing her lips together, she began **tugging** on the chains with all her considerable strength. She felt one link in the chain begin to give way and increased her efforts. Just as the chain ripped away from the wall, the door was flung open. Maegan didn't stop to think, but kept the chain moving rapidly. It landed with a **wallop** on Rory's head.

As he yelled in pain, Maegan lunged past him. Seeing her telephone on a table in the bar, she grabbed it and rushed out onto the crowded city street. It

to tug	zerren, reißen
⚡ wallop	Rums, (harter) Schlag
to dash (out)	(heraus)stürmen, (heraus)rasen
to give chase	verfolgen, hinterherrennen
leek	Lauch

was daylight, but thick clouds were blocking the morning sun. Maegan noticed a bus stopping just ahead and rushed forward to catch it. As the bus pulled away, she saw Rory **dash out** of the club. The rush-hour-filled streets meant he couldn't use his vampire speed to **give chase**, but there was no need to take chances. Bending forward in the seat so he couldn't see her, she pressed the phone's redial button.

"Gareth, that sandwich of yours is long gone. I'm not the greatest of cooks, but I could warm up some tinned **leek** soup. It's a Welsh speciality."

Talking of fate and destiny made Arianne nervous, and she wanted to change the subject.

"Maybe later, Arianne. I'm really sleepy, though. I guess vampires don't need to rest, but I could use some shut-eye. Is there a room where I could take a nap?"

Übung 23: True or false? Kreuzen Sie die korrekten Aussagen an!

1. Arianne let Caitlin and Owen go because they had realized that she had become a vampire. ❏

2. Gareth's ancestors had once worked for Arianne. ❏

3. Maegan's kidnappers treated her kindly. ❏

4. Jonas was Maegan's nephew. ❏

5. Rory planned to kill Frederick. ❏

Arianne didn't answer but, keeping his hand in hers, got up and led him towards the curving staircase in the hall. Upstairs, she opened a door that revealed one of the most beautiful rooms Gareth had ever seen. In one corner there was a sofa and two upholstered chairs grouped around a low table. The other corner was dominated by a huge canopy bed.

"Arianne, this may sound weird, but I think I'd be very uncomfortable sleeping in the same bed you shared with your husband," he admitted.

"This was – is – my room," Arianne told him. "Rhys's was

⚡ shut-eye	Schlaf, Nickerchen
upholstered	gepolstert
canopy bed	Himmelbett

through that connecting door. It was very uncommon in Victorian times for husbands and wives from the wealthier classes to share a room. Rhys never slept here. I always went to him."

Even though Arianne could no longer blush, she remembered the way her cheeks had flushed every time Rhys had requested her presence in his chamber. She had loved and desired him, but the feelings Gareth aroused in her seemed somehow more passionate and intense.

She smiled up at Gareth seductively. "Just how sleepy are you?"

Gareth read the message in her eyes and felt his exhaustion evaporating.

"Not very, but my hunger has come back in full force, and I know just exactly how I would like to satisfy it."

Arianne slid into his arms and whispered, "I'm hungry, too, Gareth, hungry for your kisses and dying to feel like a woman again."

For the first time ever, Arianne made the first move.

Gareth didn't need to be asked twice. Lifting her into his arms, he carried her over to the bed, and as they sank down upon the soft mattress, he began covering her with kisses.

to blush	erröten
to evaporate	sich in Luft auflösen, verdampfen
to graze	leicht berühren, streifen
to mingle with	sich (ver)mischen mit

Arianne moaned in delight at his caresses and placed her lips on his throat, inhaling his captivating scent.

Gareth shuddered as her teeth grazed his neck, and he raised his head to gaze into her eyes. In shock, he saw that they were completely silver and that her fangs were extending.

A wave of fear mingled with his desire, and he hesitated before going further. Would he survive making love with a vampire?

But as Arianne pulled him closer and her hands explored his body, Gareth forgot everything except the sensations her touch aroused.

Übung 24: Hidden words. Finden Sie zehn Wörter, die beschreiben, was oder wie Gareth sich fühlt!

D	Y	P	W	O	R	R	I	E	D
E	T	A	R	O	U	S	A	L	R
S	G	S	C	F	D	I	R	A	S
I	B	S	H	O	C	K	E	D	L
R	M	I	Q	L	E	D	C	H	E
E	A	O	U	H	M	L	J	U	E
Z	R	N	V	W	A	F	N	N	P
R	U	N	S	U	R	E	O	G	Y
U	E	X	A	J	U	A	P	E	L
T	I	R	E	D	M	R	I	R	A

A gusty wind was blowing across the causeway that separated Anglesey from Holy Island. Just before sunset, Frederick had parked the car near the bridge and was standing outside it, waiting. His research had paid off, and he was certain that he now knew where he would find Arianne. And thanks to Maegan's morning call, he also knew that the vampires he was waiting for were not to be trusted.

Suddenly, his nostrils flared as he caught the scent of two vampires. They were nearby, but he couldn't yet see Rory's gang members. A vibration in his coat pocket momentarily distracted him, and he reached automatically for his mobile.

"Frederick, darling, it's me again. I'm almost in position. Remember, be very careful," Meagan couldn't help warning him once more.

A slight movement to his right caught Frederick's eye. "They're here, Maegan. Stay hidden. I'll be there with Matt and Gavin soon."

Frederick hung up and slipped the phone back into his pocket. Things were about to get very interesting.

Arianne stretched **languorously** and then curled up closer to Gareth. He was sleeping deeply with a peaceful smile on his face. Poor darling, she thought, he's all tired out from our lovemaking.

Gently, she stroked his back and he stirred. She felt his arms tighten around her and let out a sigh of deep contentment.

causeway	Damm(straße)
his nostrils flared	seine Nasenflügel bebten
languorously	wohlig, schläfrig
to dawn on sb.	jmd. dämmern, jmd. aufgehen
to boot	obendrein, noch dazu

"Sleep a little bit longer, love, I'm going to go downstairs and have a quick look around."

At the sound of her voice, Gareth opened his eyes. "Did you just call me 'love', Arianne?"

"I suppose so, Gareth."

She hadn't meant to say it. The word had somehow just slipped out. But it **dawned on her** that it was true. She not only desired Gareth, she was beginning to love him. In the same moment, it was also clear to her that the situation was impossible. There was no way they could have any sort of future together. He was a human, a famous one **to boot**. She began to pull herself out of his embrace.

"I know what you're thinking, Arianne, and just stop it right now," Gareth said, turning over on top of her.

"It doesn't bother me any more that you're a vampire. Of course I don't understand everything, and I haven't had time to think about all the ramifications. But one thing is for sure: Vampire or not, you're the most fascinating woman I've ever met. I've never felt this way before, and I want to be with you."

Gareth saw the uncertainty in her eyes. "Arianne, believe me, it's as if my soul has recognized a connection between us, one that I never knew was missing from my life."

"That's the problem, Gareth. I don't have a life any more, or a soul either. It died the moment Frederick forced me to drink his blood."

Übung 25: Adjectives and adverbs. Formulieren Sie die Sätze neu, indem Sie die markierten Adjektive in Adverbien umwandeln oder umgekehrt!

1. A gusty wind was blowing across the causeway.

_____

2. Gareth was sleeping deeply .

_____

3. Arianne stretched languorously .

_____

4. Arianne let out a contented sigh.

_____

"Arianne, somehow I think you do still have a soul. And even though it no longer beats in a human way, I can feel your heart. As for your body..."

Gareth began kissing her again and let his caresses show her how he felt about her body.

ramification	Konsequenz
to dispose of sth.	etw. beseitigen
uproar	Aufruhr
the odds are in sb.'s favour	jds. Chancen stehen nicht schlecht

Arianne knew she could push Gareth away with one finger and that it would be the right course of action. Somehow, though, she could not bring herself to use her strength against him. Instead, she let herself be swept away on waves of passion.

"Good evening, Frederick. Nice set of wheels."

The shadowy figure ran his fingers along the side of the sports car.

"You're late. I was expecting you half an hour ago. And please be so kind as to get your filthy hands off my car. You haven't even introduced yourself!" Frederick snapped.

"Oh, sorry, old chap. We had to stop off for a quick, um, bite."

Gavin licked his lips at the thought of the woman they had found by accident hiking along the nearby Coastal Path.

"Now there's one less tourist spoiling the countryside," he continued. "Oh, by the way, I'm Gavin and this is Matt."

"Pleased to make your acquaintance," Frederick lied.

He could feel his fangs starting to extend. The bloody idiots! They'd killed a tourist, and he only hoped they had taken the trouble to **dispose of** the body properly. The last thing he needed was to have the local population in an **uproar**. What worried him more was the fact that Gavin and Matt had just fed. It meant if they did indeed decide to attack him, **the odds would be in their favour**.

Übung 26: Translation. Lesen Sie weiter und fügen Sie die Übersetzung der angegebenen Begriffe richtig ein!

Fahren   gehen wir   Beifahrersitz   verschwenden

befehlen   widerwillig

"All right, you two, enough time **1.** _____.

Get in the car and **2.** _____ hunting," he

3. _____. "Matt, you take the wheel, I've

done enough **4.** _____ for one day."

5. _____, Matt did as requested. Frederick

hopped into the back, and Gavin slid into the

6. _____.

4  Dark Dawn

When Gareth opened his eyes, he was alone and he realized night had fallen. A single candle flickered on the table, casting eerie shadows on the walls. Wondering where Arianne had gone, Gareth got up and collected his clothing that was scattered all about the room. Dressing quickly, he started for the stairs.

He found Arianne staring **blankly** out of a window towards the sea. Her slim shoulders were trembling. She stiffened as she felt his presence, and as she turned towards him, he saw that her lovely face was wet with tears.

"Arianne, what is it?"

"Gareth, tomorrow I want you to go back home. You deserve so much more than I can give you. And what's more, it's too dangerous for you to be with me. I will never be safe as long as Frederick is after me and that means you won't be either."

She couldn't bear to see the flash of pain in Gareth's eyes and returned her gaze towards the sound of the crashing waves.

blankly	ausdruckslos
brusque	schroff, brüsk

"Arianne, no, no, no! There is absolutely no way I'm going to leave you alone. Not now. Surely we can find a solution?"

Gareth took a step towards her, wanting to take her into his arms again.

With a **brusque** gesture, Arianne motioned him away.

"Shush, Gareth. Be quiet and stand still."

Gareth wanted to argue with her but didn't when he saw that her eyes were starting to take on that silver glow again.

The hairs on the back of Arianne's neck were tingling. Scanning the area outside the window, her sharp vision just caught the faint flickering of light on the water. It was the reflection of two headlights approaching from the distance. Abruptly, the lights vanished and Arianne practically flew to Gareth.

Before he knew what was happening, she had thrown him over her shoulder and was rushing with him out of the back door. Within seconds, they were in the stable and she threw him into the car. Gareth saw her finish transforming before his eyes. But this time, she was not a vampire in the throes of desire for him, but blazing in fury at the thought of her enemies. She was terrifyingly beautiful.

faint	schwach
in the throes of desire	in Leidenschaft entbrannt
awe	Ehrfurcht

Arianne ignored his look of awe and slammed the car door shut. "Drive, Gareth. Drive as if your life depended on it because it does."

She then left him sitting behind the wheel and was gone before he could open his mouth in protest.

Frederick parked the car half a mile down the coast road that led to Dawn's Delight.

"Leave your phones here," he commanded. "We don't want any ringtones going off at the wrong moment."

Knowing he was right, Matt and Gavin threw their phones onto the front seat and Frederick did the same. Then the three vampires got out of the car and, without making a sound, moved towards the long, curving driveway to the house. There, the three separated. Frederick glided slowly and deliberately towards the main entrance, and Gavin and Matt slipped around to the back. Excited by the coming confrontation, neither Matt nor Gavin noticed the figure partly hidden by the hedges lining the drive.

Frederick could smell her. Not Arianne's scent, but Maegan's. Hell and damnation[1], why can't she do as she's told, he thought. She's supposed to be watching the back entrance.

Ignoring the distracting thought and his mate, Frederick continued on his way.

From her **vantage point** on top of the stable, Arianne could see all four vampires. She recognized

vantage point	Aussichtspunkt
to crouch	(sich) kauern
stake	Pflock
to conquer sb.	jmd. besiegen
to perch	hocken (auf)
to pounce on sb.	über jmd. herfallen, sich auf jmd. stürzen
to emerge from	herauskommen aus

Frederick and there was Maegan **crouched** down by the hedge. The other two were strangers, but they were huge and looked like fierce fighters. Before they disappeared from view behind the house, she saw that they were fully armed. One was carrying a long wooden **stake**, the other some type of sword with a curved blade. She would never be able to **conquer** all of them.

Maegan had to act quickly before the situation got completely out of control. She'd seen Arianne dash out of the stables, and now there she was, **perched** on top, ready to **pounce on** Frederick! **Emerging from** the shadows, she whispered to her mate.

Die treffende deutsche Übersetzung für den Fluch **hell and damnation** (wörtlich: Hölle und Verdammnis) ist hier: Verdammt nochmal!

"Frederick, Frederick, this way. Arianne is down at the beach," she lied and hoped he would believe her.

In a flash, Frederick was at Maegan's side. "What the hell are you doing, Maegan?"

"I'm just trying to help. Arianne left the house about ten minutes ago, and I've been here waiting for her to return. I'll just go around back and tell Matt and Gavin," and she left Frederick standing there before he had time to protest.

Übung 27: Fill in the blanks. Lesen Sie weiter und setzen Sie die Ausdrücke in der korrekten Form ein!

| do one's best | head towards | remain still as a statue |
| escape | fall for the trick | |

Arianne **1.** _____ as she tried to comprehend Maegan's surprising words. Was there a way to **2.** _____ with Gareth after all? It seemed that Maegan was **3.** _____ to prevent a bloody battle. But could she be trusted, and would Frederick **4.** _____? It seemed so. He was starting off again, this time **5.** _____ the beach!

Gareth had no idea if it would work, but he could no longer sit hiding in the stables, not knowing what was happening outside. **Revving up the engine**, he hit the lights and sent the car **careening** through the open doors.

As the car shot outside, Arianne made a split-second decision and leapt from the stable roof, landed on top of the speeding car and somehow managed to keep her balance.

"Faster, Gareth, faster," she screamed.

Gareth heard the faint sound of Arianne's voice yelling at him and, this time, did exactly as she told him.

At the sound of the motor, Frederick spun on his heel. He **howled** in rage when he saw Arianne clinging to the spoiler on top of the ATV that was speeding directly towards him. Pulling a **double-edged** weapon from his belt, he sprung effortlessly into the air. To Gareth it seemed as if the vampire lit up by the car lamps was flying. The sight made his blood run cold. He **jerked** the steering wheel to the right, but Frederick was too fast and landed on top of the car, right next to Arianne.

"This time, you won't escape me," he hissed and, grasping the spoiler with one hand, he **plunged** the sharp wooden end of the weapon directly towards her heart.

to rev up the engine	den Motor auf-heulen lassen
to career	schlingern
to howl	heulen, jaulen
double-edged	*hier:* mit zwei scharfen Enden
to jerk	(herum)reißen
to plunge sth.	etw. stechen, rammen
to wrench sth.	etw. (mit einem Ruck) reißen
to splinter	(zer)splittern
dangling	baumelnd

Prepared for his attack, Arianne **wrenched** her body to the side and kicked out at Frederick. Instead of a death blow, the wooden stake stabbed her shoulder. Frederick pressed the stake deeper, ripping her flesh and **splintering** bone. Despite the pain, Arianne kept on kicking and sent Frederick's lower body over the edge of the roof. Gareth saw the vampire's **dangling** legs through the passenger side window.

"Hold on tight, Arianne," he yelled and began trying to shake Frederick loose from the car by driving in a rapid slalom.

Thank goodness I always insisted on doing my own stunts, he thought as the car zigzagged down the drive.

Maegan had just reached Matt and Gavin when all three were startled by the sound of the car.

The London vampires were astonished to see her, and Gavin pointed his stake at her.

"What are you doing here, Meagan, and what are you and Frederick up to?"

Maegan was thinking fast. "There's no time for explanations. Arianne's human is getting away. I'll go after him and the two of you need to get to the beach quickly – that's where Frederick is stalking Arianne. Hurry, he needs your help!"

Matt and Gavin **fell for her ruse** and, with weapons drawn, took off towards the beach.

"Remember what Rory said," Gavin reminded Matt as they ran towards the beach. "We're supposed to make sure that it looks as if Frederick and Arianne killed each other."

Übung 28: Simple past or past progressive? Lesen Sie weiter und setzen Sie die richtige Verbform ein!

Frederick **1. hang** _____ from the top of

the car. Then Arianne **2. pull** _____

the stake out of her bleeding shoulder and **3. stab**

_____ its other, metal end into the hand

Frederick **4. use** _____ to keep his balance.

The blade **5. go** _____ right through the

middle of his palm, and Arianne **6. keep** _____

it moving, slicing up all the way to Frederick's elbow.

Blood **spewed** in all directions. Screeching in rage, Frederick swung his legs up and kicked in the passenger window.

Gareth heard the glass shatter and gasped as Frederick's legs and torso appeared right beside him. Arianne was screaming at him to stop the car and get out.

"Gareth, you can't fight him. Run, please run," she cried.

Knowing she was right, Gareth desperately looked for a way out. Seeing a huge tree to the left, he aimed the car directly towards it. "Jump now, Arianne," he pleaded, knowing that time was running out.

Frederick was still half in and half out of the car when it made yet another sudden turn. He saw the tree ahead and heard the human order Arianne to jump. With a **backflip**, he catapulted himself out of the car just before it crashed into the tree.

to fall for sb.'s ruse	auf jds. List hereinfallen
to spew	heraussprudeln, spritzen
backflip	Salto rückwärts
in a daze	benommen

The airbag inflated immediately and kept Gareth from being seriously injured. **In a daze**, he noticed the door on his side of the car opening and saw the gleam of a metal blade as it pierced the protective bag. Air escaped in a hiss, freeing him from the pressure, but immediately a hand covered his mouth and strong arms shoved him aside. Something sticky fell onto his face. Blood.

Maegan came running around the house just in time to see the car crashing into a tree and Frederick flinging himself away from it. Arianne was nowhere to be seen.

Frederick had fallen hard on the ground and landed on his back. Turning his head, he saw the ATV was at a standstill, the engine still running, but steam was coming out of its damaged bonnet. He scanned the area for Arianne but could see no sign of her.

Her distinctive scent was in the air, though, mingled with smoke, dust and something else, the smell of human fear. They were close by. He started to sit up.

"Frederick, oh Frederick, you're safe," Maegan cried in relief and flung herself on top of him, **thrusting** him back onto the ground.

The gashes on his hand and arm were already closing as he angrily pushed her aside.

"Shut up, Maegan. Arianne is not strolling on the seashore. She's nearby. I have to find her and finish this once and for all."

"Well, well, well, what have we here? Two **lovebirds** or two vampires who can't manage to get a job done?"

Matt and Gavin were walking towards them from the beach with their weapons drawn.

"She's still here, you stupid idiots," Frederick roared. "Stop fooling around and get out of my way!"

"No one calls me an idiot!" Matt saw red and lunged at Frederick with his sword drawn.

Maegan threw herself between Frederick and Matt, and the sword slashed her cheek just as Gavin swung his stake like a **club** down towards Frederick's head. The four vampires were wrestling on the ground in a **free-for-all**, cursing and screaming.

This was the opportunity Arianne had been waiting for. Jamming her foot down on the accelerator pedal, she sent the car into a backwards spin on a collision course with the fighting **predators**.

The car went right through the middle of them, sending Maegan, Frederick and Gavin flying. The back wheels rolled over Matt, crushing his legs. The sounds of his agonized

to thrust	stoßen
lovebirds *pl*	Turteltauben
club	*hier:* Keule
free-for-all	(allgemeines) Gerangel
predator	Raubtier
ignition	Zündung

screams rang in their ears as Arianne and Gareth sped down the drive.

Then another noise caught their attention. The car engine was sputtering. Arianne muttered a curse. Seeing Frederick's sports car ahead, she brought the ATV to a stop. Hoping against hope that the key had been left in the ignition, Arianne jumped out of her car and into Frederick's. Yes, the key was there! Gareth was right behind her, and this time pushed her over to the passenger side.

"You've been injured, I'll drive," he said.

Übung 29: What would have happened? Vervollständigen Sie die if-Sätze!

1. If Frederick hadn't smelt Arianne's scent and Gareth's fear, he _____

   _____

2. Maegan might not have been wounded if _____

   _____

3. If the vampires hadn't started brawling, _____

   _____

4. _____

   _____ if the keys hadn't been in the ignition.

As he gathered himself off the ground, Frederick heard his car start in the distance and shook his head. Arianne was stealing his car and once more escaping his revenge.

to rant	schimpfen, wettern
with all one's might	mit aller Kraft
to send sb. on a wild goose chase	jmd. auf eine falsche Fährte locken

"This is all your fault," he ranted. "I could kill you all!"

Maegan and Gavin both started talking at once, trying to calm Frederick down, but his rage knew no bounds.

"Just shut up. You've all done enough damage for one night."

Picking up the fallen sword, he faced the other three and put its point at Matt's throat.

"I know what Rory told you and Gavin to do," Frederick hissed. "Now stop moaning, your injuries will heal soon enough – if I let you live, that is."

"Frederick, pull yourself together," Maegan pleaded. "If you kill Matt or Gavin, Rory and the other Midnight Hunters will come after us with all their might."

"She's right," Gavin said, eyeing his stake, which was lying just a few feet away. "And don't think you'll find me an easy kill."

Maegan decided to try and take control. "This isn't getting us anywhere. Gavin, you stay with Matt until he's healed himself, and then the two of you should head back to London," she directed. "Tell Rory that his plan failed and that his, um, services are no longer needed. And Frederick, love..."

Her words were cut off as Frederick removed the sword from Matt's throat and placed it directly on the back of her neck.

"I told you to shut up, Maegan, and I meant it."

With each word, Frederick pressed the sword more firmly against her skin until he drew blood.

"You've really said enough for one night and don't think for one minute that I've forgotten that you sent me on a wild goose chase," he reminded her. "But your idea for these two here is a good one. As for you, though, I want you to go home. Now."

Übung 30: Fill in the blanks. Lesen Sie weiter und ergänzen Sie die fehlenden Begriffe!

Frederick forced the sword a bit more **1.** d_____ into her neck. "And Maegan, you will stay there until I tell you **2.** o_____."

Maegan knew there was no **3.** a_____ with Frederick. So she slowly nodded her head as best she **4.** c_____ with the weapon pressed against it.

Seeing her sign of agreement, Frederick finally took the sword away. Maegan kept her head bent so that he could not see the hatred dawning in her eyes.

"As you wish, Frederick," she whispered, but even now, she was unable to help herself. "And you, my love, what will you do now?"

"Why, you silly, stupid bitch," he snarled. "I'll track Arianne and show her who her master is before I drive this stake into her heart."

Frederick swept away and left Maegan kneeling in the drive.

Gareth ran his fingers through his hair and reduced speed as they reached the limits of an island village with an absurdly long name.

"The local people shorten the name to Llanfairpwl," Arianne's voice interrupted his thoughts. "I think this would be a good place to stop for the rest of the night. We can get accommodation at a place on a quiet street nearby. The owner is, well, an old acquaintance of mine."

"Arianne, don't you think we should keep moving? After all, Frederick and the others could be close behind us."

Gareth was still shaken by their encounter with Arianne's enemies and wanted to get as far away from them as possible.

"That's true, but they won't be expecting us to stay anywhere in this area. And, Gareth, even though vampires don't get tired, I could use some time to think about what to do next," she explained.

"Oh, Arianne, how thoughtless of me. We also need to take care of your wound. Does it hurt much?" he enquired.

"No, Gareth. It's fine," she reassured him. "Vampires heal very fast."

Übung 31: Who wants what? Was wollen die einzelnen Charaktere? Ordnen Sie zu!

1. ☐ Maegan wants Frederick to...

2. ☐ Frederick wants to...

3. ☐ Gareth wants to...

4. ☐ Arianne wants to...

a) have some quiet time to plan ahead.

b) get as far away from the other vampires as possible.

c) give up his revenge.

d) continue the search alone.

proprietress	Besitzerin
regal	majestätisch
⚡ to tuck into	verschlingen, zulangen
fragrant	duftend
shapely	wohlgeformt
to bask in sth.	etw. in vollen Zügen genießen

Fifteen minutes later, Gareth and Arianne were settled into a cosy room at the B & B. The **proprietress**, a **regal**-looking woman called Mrs James, hadn't blinked an eye[i] at their showing up in the middle of the night, or at the blood on Arianne's dress.

She and Arianne had had a short but intense conversation in Welsh, which Gareth hadn't understood a word of. Then they'd hidden the car in a tiny garage before being shown upstairs. Now Gareth was **tucking into** a bowl of delicious soup while Arianne soaked in a hot bubble bath.

Gareth shook his head and smiled at the thought of a vampire – his vampire – up to her neck in warm, **fragrant** water. It was incredible, really, to be enjoying such normal, everyday things. Even after all that he'd been through in the past three days and nights, Gareth felt more at peace than he had for years.

Arianne emerged from the bath wearing a white silk dressing gown. The thin fabric clung to

> Die idiomatische Wendung **to not blink an eye** bedeutet „nicht (mal) mit der Wimper zucken", also keine Überraschung zeigen. **In the blink of an eye** bedeutet dagegen „blitzschnell".

her **shapely** curves and highlighted the paleness of her skin. All other traces of her vampire appearance were gone, and she seemed oddly vulnerable.

Gareth got up from the table, wanting nothing more than to gather her in his arms.

Arianne let him hold her, **basking in** the warmth of his body, in the tenderness of his embrace.

Übung 32: Prepositions. Lesen Sie weiter und ergänzen Sie die fehlenden Präpositionen!

It wasn't the right moment 1. _____ romance,

though, and regretfully, she pulled 2. _____ .

The two 3. _____ them needed to talk.

"Gareth, I've been thinking," she started.

"Me too, Arianne," he cut her 4. _____ gently.

"Please, let me go first."

Gareth picked her 5. _____ and carried her

6. _____ to a floral-print sofa placed conveniently

7. _____ front of a fireplace.

He added a piece of wood to the fire and joined her on the sofa. "It seems to me that you've been running from Frederick for far too long. You can never settle, never stop hiding, never, well, just be."

Arianne stamped her foot. "What choice do I have, Gareth? Should I let him catch me? It's no picnic being a vampire, and I've often thought it would be better to just, well, let him do it and be done with it. But I will not let Frederick win. I owe it to the memories of Rhys and Jonas and to myself. I won't let Frederick destroy me, or you either, for that matter."

"Arianne, I didn't mean that you should give up. What I'm trying to point out is that all these years, you've been on the defensive, just trying to hide," he said matter-of-factly. "I think **it's way past time** you went on the offensive."

Gareth leaned back on the sofa and waited for her reaction.

"Are you saying you want me to attack Frederick? Should I call him up and offer to duel with him at sundown? Gareth, you've seen, or been in, too many films! Either that or you've **gone** completely **bonkers**," she added.

"Arianne, listen to me. I know that Frederick is dangerous…"

She didn't let him finish. "Frederick is a very powerful vampire." She articulated each word slowly as if speaking to an especially **dense** child. "There's no way in the world that I could beat him in a one-on-one battle, and it wouldn't be me against just him. I don't know those other two vampires who were with him, and there is Maegan, as well."

"Yes, well, I am not so sure about her," Gareth replied. "Didn't you find it a bit weird tonight? Only Frederick directly attacked us. Maegan seemed to be more concerned with protecting Frederick, not hurting you."

It's way past time.	Es ist allerhöchste Zeit.
⚡ to go bonkers	überschnappen
⚡ dense	dämlich
⚡ thick	begriffsstutzig
under sb.'s thumb	unter jds. Fuchtel

"Hmm, that's true, and she deliberately lied to Frederick. She told him she had seen me on the beach; I suppose to try and keep him from finding us. She may have tried to help me as she once promised. But if I did anything to harm Frederick, Maegan would rip me apart."

Gareth knew she had a point and wondered about Maegan's motives. Suddenly, he had an idea.

"Arianne, have you ever talked to Maegan since your escape?"

Arianne's immediate response was an ironic laugh. Gareth really was being **thick**.

"No, of course not! She lives with Frederick and he's got her completely **under his thumb** and…"

Arianne realized she hadn't thought things through. Why not talk to her? Maegan had also loved Rhys and been a doting aunt to Jonas. Perhaps Maegan didn't know the truth about their deaths, and if confronted with the facts, she might be persuaded to help again. After all these years, it was certainly worth a try. But how?

Gareth could see that Arianne was considering his idea and did the smartest thing he could and kept quiet.

After a few minutes, Arianne grabbed his hand.

Übung 33: Word spiral. Fügen Sie die unten beschriebenen Wörter in die Wortspirale ein!

1	2	3	4	5	6	7
22	23	24	25	26	27	8
21	36	37	38	39	28	9
20	35	42	41	40	29	10
19	34	33	32	31	30	11
18	17	16	15	14	13	12

1-10: Easily hurt or wounded.

10-16: To place your arms around each other.

16-24: To come face to face with someone or something.

24-28: To have a stately, almost royal appearance.

28-35: A special dish served in Wales.

35-42: Following and trying to catch someone.

80

"In Frederick's car there were three mobiles on the seat," Arianne said. "One of them must be his, and you can bet that Maegan's number is in it."

Gareth gave her a quick kiss. "I'll be right back with the phones."

Maegan was once again on a train, once again following Frederick's orders and once again feeling miserable. I seem to **be stuck in a rut**, she thought. In that moment, her phone rang. When she saw Frederick's number displayed, she couldn't decide whether to answer it or not. In her head, the thoughts were circling in chaos.

Finally, Maegan answered with a simple, "Hello."

"It's me, Maegan. I have Frederick's phone. Can you talk?" Arianne's voice trembled slightly as she realized Frederick could be right next to Maegan.

"You! Oh, Arianne, you really have got a nerve." Maegan **was flabbergasted** and started to hang up the phone.

doting	(sehr) liebevoll, fürsorglich
to be stuck in a rut	im immer gleichen Trott gefangen sein
⚡ to be flabbergasted	völlig baff sein
deception	Täuschung, Betrug
to clear the air	reinen Tisch machen

"Maegan, wait. Please just give me a couple of minutes of your time. Are you alone?"

Her question was met with silence.

"Maegan, I beg you. All I want to do is talk to you. I promise, no tricks, no **deception**. I think the time has come for the two of us to **clear the air**. And Maegan, there are things you need to know. About Frederick."

Maegan couldn't believe it. Arianne calling her, wanting to talk as if they were still best friends, as if the past had no meaning. She hesitated, though. She did have questions.

"All right, Arianne," she finally replied. "But not on the phone. What we have to discuss is too private and too risky."

"What do you suggest?" Arianne asked, squeezing Gareth's hand.

"I'm sure you remember where I, that is Frederick and I, live," Maegan told her. "Be there tomorrow evening. I'll be alone and you'd better be, too. I'll meet you in the summer house down at the lake. Shall we say at seven?"

"No, Maegan, I think it's better if we meet on neutral ground."

"Arianne, if you want to talk, you'll have to come to me. Frederick has ordered me not to leave the house, and I can't take any more risks than I already have."

Maegan ended the call before Arianne could raise any further objections.

Übung 34: Choose the correct alternative. Lesen Sie weiter und unterstreichen Sie die richtige Variante!

Arianne **1.** gazed / gaped at the phone in her hand, **2.** wandering / wondering if it was all a **3.** trap / trade . She told Gareth that Maegan had agreed to talk, but only **4.** in person / personal , and only **5.** whether / if she came alone.

"Arianne, if you think I'm going to let you **6.** see / sea Maegan without any back-up, you're the one **7.** whose / who's gone mad."

to raise objections	Einwände erheben
⚡ to lose it	durchdrehen
should the worst come to the worst	wenn es ganz schlimm kommen sollte

Gareth was determined not to take no for an answer. "And what if Frederick is there? Have you thought about that?"

"Well, yes, Gareth, the thought has crossed my mind, but I really don't see any other way. And this means I'm going to need all the strength I can get. I still have a couple of hours until dawn, so if you'll excuse me, I'm going to dress and go out to find some, uh, dinner."

"But where will you go, this is a village? You're not going to find any wild animals here," Gareth said, trying to come to terms with what Arianne was about to do.

"Don't worry, Gareth. Mary will have an idea or two, after all she runs a Bed & Breakfast."

Arianne laughed at the look of surprise on his face.

"Mary? You mean Mrs James? Is she a vampire, too?" Gareth thought he must be losing it after all, and no wonder.

"Yes, Gareth. But you don't need to know her story. Let's just say that Mary was a great help to me. She's the one who showed me that even though it makes us weaker, vampires can live without feeding on humans."

Gareth watched her walking towards the bath where she'd left her clothes.

Did he dare? he wondered. His human body wasn't strong enough to protect her, but maybe his blood was. Could he offer Arianne the only thing he had that might help save her should the worst come to the worst?

5 Dawn Revealed

"Arianne, wait. Have you… have you ever tried room service?"

"What?" Arianne stopped in mid-stride and turned back to Gareth.

He met her eyes and reached out to her with one hand, while slowly unbuttoning his shirt with the other. He was trembling in a combination of trepidation and excitement.

As Arianne realized what Gareth had meant by 'room service', she knew that she should, that she had to refuse. But she was mesmerized by the pulse beating rapidly on his now bared throat, and she remembered how intoxicating he had tasted. Arianne felt her fangs extending and forced herself to take a step back.

"No, darling, no… I can't," she managed to say. "It's lovely of you to offer, but really… no."

"You just called me 'darling'. Please let me do this for you, for us," Gareth said seductively. "I just have one request, my darling vampire. Please be gentle with me."

Arianne's resistance was fading fast. The mere thought of Gareth's succulent blood aroused her passions almost beyond the bounds of control, and she wondered if she dared take the risk.

He wasn't going to give her much choice about it, though. Seeing that her fangs were already ex-

trepidation	Beklommenheit
bared	entblößt
succulent	wohlschmeckend, saftig

tended, Gareth leaned in closer and pressed her lips directly onto his naked throat.

"Take me now, Arianne. I know you won't harm me. I trust you. And I want to be yours in this way, too," Gareth breathed as he cradled her towards him.

He closed his eyes, not knowing whether to expect pain, pleasure or both. As Arianne's fangs pierced his sensitive skin, he thought he might hyperventilate. What was he doing? Then he heard Arianne moan, and

to cradle sb.	jmd. zärtlich halten
soothing	beruhigend
boneless	*hier*: total entspannt

a million sensations began rushing through his body at once. Gareth let himself fall freely as his life's blood, his very essence, flowed into Arianne's mouth and satisfied them both.

Music filled the room as Arianne let her slender fingers glide one last time over the strings of the harp. As the beautiful, soothing tones faded, Gareth opened his eyes and smiled at her. Arianne left the instrument Mary had lent her and joined Gareth on the bed.

Tentatively, he touched his throat but could feel no sign of a bite wound. Had he dreamt it all?

Arianne saw his confusion. "No, darling, it wasn't a dream. You gave me the most precious of all gifts."

Slowly, she bent down to kiss the place on his neck from which she had fed.

"How are you feeling?"

Gareth gasped as her lips softly caressed his skin.

"I feel, well, I don't know how to put it," he said after a moment. "A little bit tired but completely relaxed, almost boneless. I can't say that the experience of having you drink from me was better than making love, but it was, well, extremely fulfilling. And you,

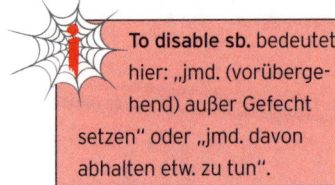

To disable sb. bedeutet hier: „jmd. (vorüberge-hend) außer Gefecht setzen" oder „jmd. davon abhalten etw. zu tun".

Arianne, how do you feel? No regrets, I hope?"

"No, darling, no regrets," she assured him. "I feel strong and happy and ready for whatever this night will bring."

The grandfather clock in the hallway chimed 2 p.m. It was time to leave for Newport and Frederick and Maegan's estate.

"Arianne, I'm going with you," Gareth said and grabbed her hand. "I know you think it's too dangerous, or that I will just be in the way. But please, let me travel as far as Newport with you. I promise I'll stay in the car while you meet with Maegan. I just can't stand the thought of waiting here, not knowing what's happening."

Arianne considered his demand. It was tempting, and they would be sure of having a few more hours together.

"All right, Gareth," she agreed. "But I'm warning you now: if you try to follow me or interfere, I will have to disable you. If it comes to a battle, I can't be distracted by trying to protect you."

Determinedly, she sat up and pulled him up by his arms. Reaching down to the floor, she picked up a long, wooden case.

"You can carry this down to the car. I'll just say goodbye to Mary, and then I'll meet you in the garage."

Übung 35: Translation. Übersetzen Sie!

1. intoxicating _____

2. mesmerized _____

3. succulent _____

4. trepidation _____

That night, Arianne **concealed** Frederick's car in a **grove** of trees across the lake from Frederick's estate.

"Remember, Gareth, don't leave the car, no matter what," she said urgently and gave him a quick kiss.

to chime	schlagen, läuten
to conceal sth.	etw. verstecken
grove	Baumgruppe
urge	Drang
unruly	widerspenstig
agenda	*hier*: Absicht, Plan

Taking one last look at his handsome face, she removed a gleaming sword from Mary's case, and then gave Gareth the phone and final instructions.

"Call me if something goes wrong and remember, stay here and wait for me. I'll be back soon."

Resisting the **urge** to kiss him again, Arianne tenderly brushed a lock of his **unruly** hair away from his cheek and slipped out of the car. Fastening the sword to the belt under her coat, she vanished into the night just as clouds covered the moon.

"Good evening, Arianne."

The calm, quiet greeting came with no warning from a corner of the summer house by the lake. Arianne turned and saw Maegan sitting on a bench, dressed completely in black. Checking that her sword could not be seen, Arianne slowly walked up the three steps that led inside and held out her hand to the shadowy figure, hoping Maegan would take it. Rising slowly, Maegan accepted, and as their fingers touched, she spoke in a rushed, worried voice.

"We don't have much time, Arianne. I have no idea where Frederick is, but he could turn up any minute. I don't know – or care – what your **agenda** is. The only reason I agreed to see you is I want you to tell me exactly what happened the night he turned you, the night when Rhys and Jonas died."

Maegan's face gave no hint of the **turmoil raging** inside her. She had to know the truth about the night of the shipwreck. Frederick wouldn't tell her, and Arianne was the only other remaining witness.

"Fine, Maegan, but you are not going to like it, perhaps you should sit down again."

"Don't concern yourself with my feelings, Arianne, just tell me."

Frederick had **combed** Holy Island and Anglesey for hours, hoping luck would be with him, and he'd find Arianne. Finally accepting the fact that she had disappeared without a trace, he decided his only alternative was to **start** his search **from scratch**. The best place to do that was from home, using all the high-tech equipment available there.

That's how he'd found her the first time, a **fluke**, really. He'd been surfing the net for music and found a piece for the harp by a mysterious composer. His curiosity aroused and with all the time in the world on his hands, he'd started digging, and his **quest** had led him to Arianne's door. He would be successful again, and then she would beg for mercy before he killed her.

turmoil	Tumult
to rage	toben, wüten
to comb	*hier*: durchkämmen, suchen
⚡ to start (sth.) from scratch	(wieder) ganz von vorne anfangen
⚡ fluke	glücklicher Zufall
quest	Suche, Streben
to ripple	(sich) kräuseln
to quiver	zittern

"It can't be," Frederick now muttered as he spotted a car – his car – parked amongst the willow trees by his estate.

He had gone in the house, where Maegan was nowhere to be seen, and had immediately left to try and locate her. He'd found something much, much better instead.

Übung 36: Unscramble. Lesen Sie weiter und ordnen Sie die Buchstaben zu sinnvollen Wörtern!

Gareth **1.** tifdesh _____ restlessly in his seat.

Outside the wind picked up, causing waves to **ripple** on the lake. It was so hard doing **2.** tonginh _____.

He opened the door and was just **3.** ragstint _____

to get out when a fist **4.** dolcdeil _____ with his

forehead. Blood began **5.** glirtinck _____ down

into his right eye, and he heard an evil laugh before he

6. labdeck _____ out.

"I suppose the best place to start is with the voyage," Arianne told Maegan softly. "Do you remember? Rhys took Jonas and me with him on a short business trip to Ireland. You'd planned to come as well, Maegan, and I didn't understand what made you change your mind, especially as Frederick was also on board. But later, afterwards...," Arianne's voice was **quivering**, and she stopped speaking.

Maegan finished Arianne's unspoken words. "Later you realized that Frederick had already turned me. I wasn't able to travel with you because the risk of my attacking a passenger was too great."

"Well, shortly after the ship set sail, a storm came up, and Jonas started feeling unwell. Rhys took him to our cabin to rest while I had a walk around on the deck. After a while, I decided to go to the cabin as well. But Frederick had got there first."

Arianne's eyes filled with tears as she remembered what had happened next. "I will never forget opening the cabin door and seeing Rhys and Jonas lying unconscious on the floor. Rhys was bleeding, but both of them were still alive when I found them. As I rushed inside, Frederick grabbed me from behind and ripped the front of my blouse. As his fangs sank into my throat, I heard Rhys moan, and Frederick stopped for an instant and forced me to open my eyes and look at my family."

Arianne could barely speak through the tears.

Übung 37: Unscramble the dialogue. Lesen Sie weiter, indem Sie die folgenden Sätze in die richtige Reihenfolge bringen!

a) "You mean Frederick's price for not killing my brother and nephew was you agreeing to let him turn you?"

b) "Frederick promised me that if I offered him the rest of my blood and then drank his, he would spare Rhys and Jonas."

c) "I was so scared, Maegan, and Frederick kept saying over and over: 'Drink, Arianne, drink from me, and I will let them live'. And so I did it, Maegan. I gave him what he wanted."

d) Maegan shook her head in disbelief and felt tears in her own eyes.

1	2	3	4

Shuddering at the memory, Arianne forced herself to go on. "And then he slashed his wrist and trickled blood into my throat. As I swallowed it, Rhys opened his eyes, and I saw the horror in them. I fell on the cabin floor, **writhing** in the agony of becoming a vampire while my husband watched. That's when Frederick began to feed first from Rhys and then from Jonas. Before he had drained them completely, he pushed my head towards their bodies and tried to make me drink from them, too."

to writhe	sich winden
to toss around sth.	etw. hin und her werfen
heart-wrenching	herzzerreißend
devastated	am Boden zerstört
revelation	Enthüllung

Arianne paused. "And, Maegan, the worst thing is that if the storm hadn't begun **tossing** the ship **around** at that very moment, I would have done it. As a newborn vampire, I would have fed on my own husband and child! For that alone, I can never forgive myself."

Arianne's tears turned to **heart-wrenching** sobs, and she buried her face in her hands.

Maegan was **devastated** by the **revelations**, but still managed to put a comforting arm around Arianne's shoulder.

"Shush, Arianne, shush," Maegan tried to soothe her. "You didn't do it. And, Arianne, you had no choice, you were powerless, just as I was."

After a moment, Maegan continued, "I will never forget him arriving here with you slung over his shoulder, both of you soaking wet. When he told me that Rhys and Jonas had died at sea, I believed him. What I couldn't quite swallow was his version of why he had turned you. I knew that he desired you, but when he seduced me into being his donor and then turned me, I thought it meant he loved me. But when he brought you here, I saw that he only had eyes for you. That's why I helped you escape."

| abode | Bleibe |

"But why didn't you..."

Arianne stopped her question abruptly. Maegan's phone was ringing. Maegan gave a low moan when she saw the name on the display. Before answering, she showed the caller ID to Arianne.

"Maegan, my dear, I'm so delighted to hear your voice. I was worried when I arrived and discovered you weren't at home. But I expect you have a good explanation for that, don't you, love?"

Arianne could hear Frederick's honeyed words clearly and motioned for Maegan to give her the mobile.

"Frederick. Stop playing mind-games. How did you get your phone back and where is Gareth?"

"Oh, Arianne, how nice to talk to you at last," Frederick replied with his evil laugh. "Anyway, I'm not playing games, believe me. Your human is just fine – for the moment, that is."

"What have you done with him?" Arianne feared the worst.

"Funnily enough, Arianne, you could say your Gareth looks a bit like Rhys did, just before he departed this world. You can rush right up the hill to his rescue. I can't wait to welcome you back to my lovely abode. Oh, and Arianne, you'd better hurry. He's bleeding, and I am starting to get hungry," he laughed wickedly.

Her fangs were out as Arianne let the phone slide out of her hand and drew her sword. Hearing Maegan's gasp of surprise, Arianne swung towards the other vampire.

"Frederick has Gareth and I'm going after him."

Maegan grabbed Arianne's arm. "You know it's a trap. Frederick will kill your human, just as he killed my brother and Jonas. Then he will kill you. Is your Gareth really worth it?"

Arianne fixed her with a cold stare. "Yes, he is. The real question, Maegan, is for you. Is Frederick worth all that you've done for him in all these years?"

Übung 38: Crossword puzzle. Lösen Sie das Kreuzworträtsel!

Across

4. If you pass out, you are...
7. A major, often shocking fact that people are made aware of is a...
8. Frederick made one to Arianne, but he broke it.

Down

1. To jump suddenly, like an attacking cat – or vampire.
2. A humorous term for the place where somebody lives.
3. Vampires scream like this when they are furious.
5. When a story is difficult to believe, it is hard to...
6. A vampire's teeth are called...

Without waiting for a reply, Arianne sprinted towards the house as the wind began to howl, and the first raindrops fell from the dark sky above. This time, Frederick would not have an easy victory.

Gareth moaned as he came to his senses. He was standing with his back pressed firmly against a hard, cold surface. He tried to move, but thick ropes were binding him around the chest and legs. He could feel rain beating down on his face, and behind the **gag** someone had put between his lips, he could taste blood. When he tried to open his eyes, he realized in horror that he was blindfolded as well. He had never felt so helpless.

Gareth's heart pounded rapidly in fear. He thought that he could sense a presence **lurking** nearby, but maybe that was just his imagination running wild. Still, he was sure that it had been Frederick who had captured him, and now he was being used as **bait** to trap Arianne! Desperately, Gareth tried to think of a way to escape. What did the heroes always do in the films when they got into such **predicaments**?

gag	*hier*: Knebel
to lurk	lauern
bait	Köder
predicament	Notlage
wrought-iron	schmiedeeisern
to peer	spähen, blicken

A familiar weight on his right thigh made him remember the penknife he'd taken from his rucksack a lifetime ago back at the garage in Cardiff. Praying his captor wasn't watching him, Gareth slowly and carefully began to manoeuvre his jacket beneath the ropes so he could get at the knife.

Arianne stopped suddenly when she reached the **wrought-iron** gates that closed off the back garden of Frederick's estate.
Tightening her grip on the sword, she **peered** through them, all her powerful senses on red alert. The garden was filled with

statues of mystical creatures positioned in a huge circle around the central lawn. Sporadic groups of flowers, **shrubs** and trees swaying in the wind cast eerily moving shadows.

shrub	Strauch
gingerly	vorsichtig
to creep	kriechen
marble	Marmor

There was no sign of Frederick or of Gareth, though, and she **gingerly** pushed open the gates and **crept** through them, knowing each step was taking her closer to Frederick's attack. She could not catch his scent, but the wind could be carrying it away from her.

Then she saw something, a tiny movement on the edge of the lawn. It seemed as if one of the statues was coming to life! But no, there was a darker shape outlined against the pale **marble**. It was Gareth tied to the statue, and he was alive!

Übung 39: Fill in the verbs. Lesen Sie weiter und setzen Sie die folgenden Verben richtig ein!

dash   hiding   risk   remain   scanned

She wanted to **1.** _____ towards him immediately but forced herself to **2.** _____ calm. Where was Frederick? She **3.** _____ the gloomy garden again, but there were so many places he could be **4.** _____ . She would just have to **5.** _____ it, Arianne thought.

Frederick had had his eyes trained on Arianne ever since she'd arrived. With sadistic pleasure, he saw her realize that her lover was tied to his favourite work, the sculpture of an ancient god of death. He delighted in her hesitation, certain she would not notice him perched high above her in the oak tree. In wicked **glee**, he watched as she began running towards the man he'd taken prisoner.

At last, he thought, and prepared to pounce.

Arianne's keen vampire senses still did not pick up any trace of Frederick, but she knew that he must be watching her and would be expecting her to **make a beeline for** Gareth. She began sprinting towards the statue, but then leapt suddenly to the right as she noticed Frederick, with sword I hand, jump from a tree.

glee	Entzücken
⚡ to make a beeline for sth.	schnurstracks auf etw. zulaufen
evasive	ausweichend
to hurl	schleudern
to jackknife	eine Bewegung wie ein Klappmesser machen
lethal blow	Todesstoß
to stagger	wanken

Arianne's sudden **evasive** move had put her just inches out of his reach. He lunged towards her and she lashed out with her weapon. Frederick parried, and the two blades crashed together in mid-air. Frederick was taller and the more experienced fighter. He pulled back for another blow, and as Arianne lunged at him, he grabbed her with his free hand and **hurled** her into the air.

Landing hard on her back on the grass, Arianne rolled to her side, trying to leap to her feet. Frederick was already on her, though, and caught her foot with his right hand, holding her fast. Arianne immediately **jackknifed** into a sitting position and brought the sword down on Frederick's head. But she was in no position to give him the **lethal blow**.

Wondering at the speed and strength of the counter-attack, Frederick roared as he let go of her foot to take his own sword in both hands.

As his grip loosened, Arianne jumped up and raced towards Gareth.

The sounds of clashing swords and Frederick's howl startled Gareth. Was Arianne battling Frederick? The very[i] thought made Gareth increase his efforts to free himself.

> **Very** wird hier nicht als verstärkendes Adverb (sehr) verwendet, sondern - vor dem Substantiv - als attributives Adjektiv. **The very thought** heißt: „der bloße Gedanke/allein der Gedanke". Very kann auch „genau" bedeuten: at this very minute - genau in dieser Minute

The penknife was small but incredibly sharp, and he could feel the rope around him beginning to give way. Just as the knife cut the last thread, he heard Arianne's voice.

"Gareth, get ready," she screamed.

Then suddenly he heard a blade strike stone, and the remaining ropes fell off. Arianne must have sliced through them from behind.

Gareth ripped off his blindfold as she picked him up and started running back towards the garden gates.

The slight delay caused by her rescuing Gareth was all the time Frederick needed to catch up. With one last powerful leap, he was upon them. He grabbed Arianne around the neck with one hand and slashed at her with the sword in his other.

She tried to keep moving, but the force of Frederick's attack made her **stagger**. Just before she crashed to the ground, she managed to toss Gareth aside and free up her hands so she could use her sword. Frederick saw her reaching for the weapon and shoved her face down onto the grass.

Übung 40: Correct the mistakes. Lesen Sie weiter und korrigieren Sie die sechs Fehler im folgenden Absatz!

The sword fell unto the grass beside her, and Frederick kicked it away. He snatched her buy the hair and pulled her head back so forceful, she thought he would tear it of. Arianne was bleeding heavily from them sword wounds, but she kicked out and landed a blow too his **groin**.

1. _____   4. _____

2. _____   5. _____

3. _____   6. _____

Howling **ferociously**, Frederick yanked her over onto her back. Before she could try and roll away, he jumped on her stomach, and Arianne was practically immobilized.

Towering above her, Frederick drew the point of the sword lightly down her cheek, **leaving** a fresh trail of blood **in its wake**. Removing the blood-tipped sword from her face, he held it against her neck and fixed her with a penetrating, silver stare of pure hatred.

"Prepare to die, Arianne," he hissed, "and let your final thought be that as soon as you are gone, I will make a celebratory feast of your boyfriend."

groin	Leistengegend
ferociously	wild
to leave sth. in one's wake	etw. hinter sich zurücklassen

Winded from the fall and lying just a few feet away, Gareth saw that Frederick had Arianne trapped. His fear of the **dastardly** vampire turned into a white-hot rage. He knew it was fruitless, that Frederick was going to kill him anyway. But maybe he could give Arianne a chance to escape.

Hurling himself forward, Gareth **head-butted** Frederick in the side while swinging up the penknife he was still clutching. It was like running into a brick wall, and Frederick remained standing on Arianne's stomach. Gareth staggered back. The knife, though, hit home and **skewered** Frederick's left eye. The vampire jerked back and reached out to cover the gaping wound with one hand. With the other, he swung the sword furiously at Gareth.

winded	außer Atem
dastardly	hinterhältig
to head-butt sb.	jmd. einen Kopfstoß versetzen
to skewer	aufspießen
to let up	nachlassen, aufhören
to wrest sth. from sb.	jmd. etw. entreißen
to protrude	herausragen

The instant the pressure from Frederick's sword **let up**, Arianne threw him off and grabbed his blade with her bare hands.

"Get the hell out of here, Gareth," she screamed in desperation as Frederick tried to **wrest** the sword **from** her hands, sending it deeper into her now-bleeding palms.

Then out of the darkness something whizzed right past her ear. Frederick gasped and suddenly stopped struggling. His fingers slipped off the sword, and he slowly sank to the ground, staring with disbelief at the shaft of an arrow **protruding** from his chest.

Arianne had no idea if the arrow had a wooden head that would be enough to finish him off. With a slight, decisive nod, she positioned the sword, ready to behead him.

"No, Arianne. He belongs to me!"

Frederick's eyelids fluttered at the sound of the voice carrying across his garden. It couldn't be!

"Maegan," he whispered. "Why...?"

And then she was upon him, a bow slung across her shoulder and a stake in her hand. She pushed Arianne aside, looked down at her mate and, with no warning, plunged the stake into his heart.

Just before the silver light left his eye forever, she looked down at him and answered his final question.

"Because you killed Rhys and Jonas and...," the tears raining down her face mingling with Frederick's blood, she finished, "… you never loved me."

Then she crumbled in a sobbing heap onto his lifeless body.

Übung 41: True or false? Kreuzen Sie die richtigen Aussagen an!

1. Approaching the garden, Arianne immediately knows where Frederick is hiding. ❑

2. Gareth manages to partially free himself using the penknife. ❑

3. Arianne's defensive manoeuvres leave Frederick severely wounded. ❑

4. Gareth has given up all hope of staying alive when he attacks Frederick. ❑

5. Maegan has mixed emotions about having killed Frederick. ❑

Gareth sank to his knees, trembling in shock and relief that the battle was finally over.

Frederick was no more and, above all, Arianne was safe. Slowly, he stood up again, wanting to go to her and take her in

grieving	trauernd
nestled in	gekuschelt in
to fathom sth.	etw. begreifen
by mutual consent	in gegenseitigem Einverständnis

his arms, but he stopped when he saw her reach out to Maegan and help the **grieving** vampire to her feet.

"Maegan," Arianne said softly, "I... what you did just now... I don't think I will ever be able to thank you enough."

Maegan gazed at her with empty eyes. "I didn't do it for you, Arianne. It was the only way. I could never have let Frederick live after finding out what he did and I..."

Maegan could not go on.

Arianne reached out to comfort her, about to ask her if there was anything she could do, but Meagan shrugged her off.

"No, don't. It's best if you leave now. I need some time on my own." With a glance at Gareth, Maegan continued, "You have, well, other concerns. Take Frederick's car. He won't be needing it any more. Farewell, Arianne."

Nestled in Gareth's arms twelve hours later, Arianne still could not **fathom** [i] that the nightmare was finally over. They had left as Maegan requested and, **by mutual consent**, returned to Dawn's Delight and gone directly to bed. Exhausted and shaken by all that had happened, Gareth had fallen into a deep sleep as soon as his head hit the pillow.

> Das Verb **to fathom** ist abgeleitet vom nautischen Maß **fathom** (Faden = 1,8 m) zur Bestimmung der Wassertiefe. Daran angelehnt kann das Verb auch „etw. ausloten" bedeuten.

Arianne smiled to herself, enjoying the sensation of the steady rise and fall of his chest against her naked back, and let one hand reach down to caress his thigh. Gareth stirred restlessly in his sleep, and Arianne turned in his arms to gather him tightly in her own.

"Shh. It's all right, darling," she said softly. "Everything's fine now."

As she gazed at his troubled face, Gareth opened his eyes, and she saw that they were moist with unshed tears.

"Oh Arianne, oh my love, I dreamed I had lost you," Gareth said with a choked voice as he fought back the tears. "I thought Frederick was going to behead you right in front of my eyes and I would be powerless to stop him."

foolhardy	verwegen, töricht
all-consuming	alles verzehrend
luscious	sinnlich, voll
cushy	bequem

"But you did stop him, Gareth," she said, gently stroking his back with one hand. "Attacking Frederick with only that tiny penknife was so selfless, so brave, and," Arianne couldn't help adding, "so incredibly **foolhardy**. How dare you risk your life like that?"

Gareth cupped her exquisite face in his hands. "Arianne, I love you, and without you, I don't know that I would have a life. You mean everything to me. Just the thought of being without you, not being able to hold you, is unbearable. I love you."

He lowered his lips to hers.

As they kissed, Arianne let the waves of love she felt for Gareth wash over her. His hands were now sliding down her body, and she arched her back, trying to get as close to him as possible. Her feelings for him were **all-consuming**, and she wanted nothing more than to never leave this bed, this moment and this man.

Übung 42: Verb forms. Lesen Sie weiter und ergänzen Sie die korrekten Verbformen!

Their embrace **1. interrupt** _____ by the shrill tone of a ringing phone.

It **2. come** _____ from Gareth's rucksack, which he'd left on the floor across the room. As Gareth **3. start** _____ to get up, Arianne pulled him back towards her.

" **4. ignore** _____ it, my darling. I can think of much more pleasurable things to do than talking on the phone," she **5. tempt** _____ him.

"Me too, Arianne," he agreed and ran his finger across her **luscious** lips. "But I expect it's my agent calling. I've been out of touch with my office for days now, and I expect he's going out of his mind worrying what I've been up to."

Gareth pulled himself out of her arms and grinned. "Don't you worry, I promise not to tell him, and I'll keep it short."

With a tiny frustrated sigh, Arianne sank back into the **cushy** pillows and let her eyes follow Gareth's muscular body as he crossed the room. He really is divinely gorgeous, she thought and smiled in anticipation of the pleasures to come. Her smile disappeared, though, as she listened to Gareth's conversation.

He had an entirely different life of his own across the ocean, she realized. He was talented, famous and human, and there was no room in his world for a vampire. Theirs must be a love until dawn, and after that, she would have to find a way to go on without Gareth.

She sat up, **chastising herself** for daring to dream that they would somehow have a future.

"Fantastic, we'll talk again tomorrow," Gareth ended his call and **bounded** across the room, back into bed.

He noticed immediately that Arianne's mood had changed.

"Arianne, what is it? Are you **miffed** at me for accepting the call?"

"No, Gareth, it's just reminded me of who you are and who, or what, I am. I don't know how we can ever make things work between us," she said in despair and buried her face in her hands.

"But I know how, Arianne," he told her and lifted her chin so that he could see into her silver-tinged eyes.

to chastise sb.	jmd. schelten
to bound	springen
⚡ miffed	verstimmt, verärgert
limelight	Rampenlicht

Taking her hands, Gareth posed the question he'd been dying to ask. "Arianne, will you come with me to the States?"

Arianne was taken completely aback at his request and began to list all the reasons why it could never work.

"You live in the **limelight**, Gareth, how could I ever fit in, and..."

Gareth cut her off by covering her lips firmly with his own and pressing her back onto the bed. He deepened the kiss, and Arianne wrapped her arms around him, moaning in pleasure. Her mounting desire for Gareth replaced some of her doubts with the hope that perhaps their love could last beyond dawn.

Sometimes actions were more convincing than words, and Gareth was very, very good at persuasion.

Abschlusstest

Übung 1: Questions to the text. Beantworten Sie die Fragen zum Text!

1. Which characters do we know for sure come from Wales?

_____

2. How did Frederick use Gareth as bait to trap Arianne?

_____

_____

3. How do, or did, Arianne, Gareth, Mary and Rhys earn their keep?

_____

_____

4. Why did Arianne think that her relationship with Gareth was just a love until dawn?

_____

_____

Übung 2: Crossword puzzle. Lösen Sie das Kreuzworträtsel!

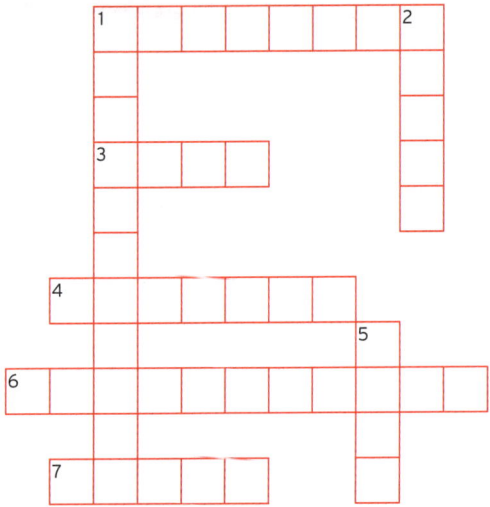

Across

1. To stick out from something.
3. The opposite of dawn.
4. The heroine of "Love Until Dawn" is a...
6. The feeling of anxiety and fear.
7. The weapon of choice to kill a vampire.

Down

1. A troubling situation.
2. Arianne's hair is as black as...
5. Just manage to escape in the ... of time.

Übung 3: Phrasal verbs. Bilden Sie Phrasal Verbs und ordnen Sie die passende Definition zu!

1. ☐ snoop   _____   **a)** make sense

2. ☐ pass   _____   **b)** focus directly

3. ☐ train   _____   **c)** end sb.'s life violently

4. ☐ add   _____   **d)** search secretly

5. ☐ do sb.   _____   **e)** faint

Übung 4: Odd one out. Welches Wort ist das „schwarze Schaf"? Unterstreichen Sie das nicht in die Reihe passende Wort!

1. traipse   stride   bound   perch

2. vicious   ferocious   luscious   malicious

3. chide   snicker   scold   chastise

4. thrust   wrest   yank   grab

Übung 5: Idiomatic expressions. Vervollständigen Sie die Idioms!

1. He keeps things under _____.

2. She needed to keep her _____ about her.

3. You don't say anything, has the _____?

4. An unconscious person is out _____.

Übung 6: British and American English. Vervollständigen Sie die Tabelle!

	German	British	American
1.	_____	_____	buckle up
2.	Hosen	_____	_____
3.	Urlaub	_____	_____
4.	rumknutschen	_____	_____
5.	Motorhaube	_____	_____

Übung 7: Say it again. Benutzen Sie die vorgegebenen Wörter und schreiben Sie die Sätze neu!

1. This is Gareth's first visit to Wales. never

_____

2. Caitlin was employed by Arianne. used to / work

_____

3. Arianne borrowed a sword from Mary. lend

_____

4. Maegan lied blatantly to Frederick. tell

_____

5. Arianna was close to tears. verge

_____

Übung 8: Translation quiz. Übersetzen Sie und enträtseln Sie das Lösungswort!

1. verdampfen __ ☐ __ __ __ __ __ __

2. Bleibe ☐ __ __ __ __

3. Rampenlicht __ __ ☐ __ __ __ __ __

4. sich kräuseln __ __ ☐ __ __ __

5. Köder __ __ ☐ __

6. sich entkleiden __ __ __ ☐ __ __ __

7. schlingern __ __ __ ☐ __ __

8. nachdenklich __ __ __ ☐ __ __ __

Lösung: ☐ ☐ ☐ ☐ ☐ ☐ ☐ ☐

Lösungen

Übung 1: 1. c 2. d 3. a 4. e 5. b

Übung 2: 1. sensed 2. had gone 3. knew 4. had not seen 5. began

Übung 3: 1. falsch (She knows he hasn't seen her.)
2. richtig 3. falsch (Her voice is muffled.)
4. falsch (She isn't sure whether she has really seen him before.)

Übung 4: 1. scolds 2. dazzling 3. ignorant 4. pale 5. waist 6. ravishing
Lösung: caress

Übung 5: 1. control 2. keep 3. instincts 4. feast 5. struggle 6. sense

Übung 6: 1. angrily 2. obsessively 3. gentle 4. wickedly

Übung 7: 1. No, it weakens her.
2. No, she's fairly confident that he won't remember.
3. No, he didn't move once.
4. No, he woke up because she was patting (slapping) his face.

Übung 8: 1. came/got to his feet 2. rescuer/saviour 3. managed 4. distracted 5. whiff 6. seemed familiar

Übung 9: 1. rings a bell 2. pitch-dark 3. giggle 4. belt up

Übung 10: 1. For work purposes, Arianne uses a pseudonym.
2. Arianne decided to stick to the truth.
3. She earns her keep as a composer.
4. If Gareth's memory serves, a man composed the film's score.

Übung 11: 1. spent 2. getting 3. explained 4. had come 5. needed 6. I've always wanted 7. it's been

Übung 12: 1. Her cottage stands in Pentyrch Village, on the outskirts to Cardiff.
2. Because his feelings for her have made him warm.
3. She rushes away because she sees that the curtains are slightly open.
4. He sees her silver eyes and fangs.

Übung 13: 1. If Gareth jumps out of the car, he might be killed.
2. If Arianne had wanted to kill Gareth, she could have done it in the cave.
3. If Maegan hadn't opened the curtains, Arianne would have had no warning.
4. If Frederick finds Arianne, he will try to kill her.

Übung 14: 1. came 2. plausible 3. Perhaps 4. suppose 5. minute 6. be

Übung 15: 1. Arianne's address book was found in a drawer.
2. The first rule of vampire safety has been broken.
3. A couple of his strongest vampires should be sent to Anglesey Island.
4. They might be let in on the kill.

Übung 16: 1. plan 2. clear 3. get on 4. option 5. here and now 6. way

Übung 17: 1. draw in a breath 2. let go of 3. keep out of harm's way 4. carry on with 5. brace oneself

Übung 18: „Das ist nicht lustig", unterbrach Maegan. „Es sieht aus, als ob Arianne nicht nur endlich wieder aufgetaucht ist, sie hat auch einen Menschen bei sich. Einen Mann. Frederick ist sich sicher, dass sie ihn als Spender benutzt, und ihm wahrscheinlich alles über das Vampirsein und über unsere Welt erzählt hat. Ihr alle kennt die Strafe dafür! Ich finde es gar nicht witzig/zum Lachen."

Übung 19: 1. exactly 2. subject 3. curious 4. ready 5. give

Übung 20: 1. Gareth said that he wanted to know about their hideaway.
2. Arianne told him the house was just outside a village called Rhoscolyn.
3. She said that she didn't think so, but couldn't be certain.
4. He replied that it sounded as if Maegan couldn't be in the picture.

Übung 21: 1. concerned (worried) 2. tied up (busy) 3. to be up to (to plan) 4. childish games (silliness) 5. Raising his voice (speak louder)

Übung 22: 1. are 2. have 3. was 4. to keep 5. would have done 6. was suffering

Übung 23: 1. falsch (She was afraid she would feed on them and/or that they would find out.) 2. richtig
3. falsch (They tortured and chained her.) 4. richtig
5. richtig

Übung 24:

D	Y	P	W	O	R	R	I	E	D
E	T	A	R	O	U	S	A	L	R
S	G	S	C	F	D	I	R	A	S
I	B	S	H	O	C	K	E	D	L
R	M	I	Q	L	E	D	C	H	E
E	A	O	U	H	M	L	J	U	E
Z	R	N	V	W	A	F	N	N	P
R	U	N	S	U	R	E	O	G	Y
U	E	X	A	J	U	A	P	E	L
T	I	R	E	D	M	R	I	R	A

Übung 25: 1. A wind was blowing gustily across the causeway.
2. Gareth was in a deep sleep.
3. Arianne gave a languorous stretch.
4. Arianne sighed contentedly.

Übung 26: 1. has been wasted 2. let's go 3. commanded/ordered 4. driving 5. Reluctantly 6. passenger seat

Übung 27: 1. remained still as a statue 2. escape 3. doing her best 4. fall for the trick 5. heading towards

Übung 28: 1. was hanging 2. pulled 3. stabbed 4. was using 5. went 6. kept

Übung 29: 1. ...would/might not have known they were still there.
2. ...she hadn't thrown herself between Matt and Frederick.
3. ...Arianne and Gareth might not have been able to escape.
4. They couldn't have used Frederick's car to escape...

Übung 30: 1. deeply 2. otherwise 3. arguing 4. could

Übung 31: 1. c 2. d 3. b 4. a

Übung 32: 1. for 2. away 3. of 4. off 5. up 6. over 7. in

Übung 33:

1 V	2 U	3 L	4 N	5 E	6 R	7 A
22 T	23 E	24 R	25 E	26 G	27 A	8 B
21 N	36 U	37 R	38 S	39 U	28 L	9 L
20 U	35 P	42 G	41 N	40 I	29 E	10 E
19 O	34 U	33 O	32 S	31 K	30 E	11 M
18 C	17 N	16 E	15 C	14 A	13 R	12 B

Übung 34: 1. gazed 2. wondering 3. trap 4. in person 5. if 6. see 7. who's

Übung 35: 1. berauschend 2. gebannt 3. wohlschmeckend 4. Beklommenheit

Übung 36: 1. shifted 2. nothing 3. starting 4. collided 5. trickling 6. blacked

Übung 37: 1. b 2. d 3. a 4. c

Übung 38:

Crossword solution:
- 1 (down): P O U N C E
- 2 (down): A B ...
- 3 (down): H W L
- 4 (across): U N C O N S C I O U S
- 5 (down): S W A L ... O
- 6 (down): F A N G S
- 7 (across): R E V E L A T I O N
- 8 (across): V O W

Übung 39: 1. dash 2. remain 3. scanned 4. hiding 5. risk

Übung 40: 1. onto (unto) 2. by (buy) 3. forcefully (forceful)
4. off (of) 5. the (them) 6. to (too)

Übung 41: 1. falsch (She doesn't know where he is.) 2. richtig
3. falsch (She causes him some pain, but never
disables him.) 4. richtig 5. richtig

Übung 42: 1. was interrupted 2. was coming 3. started
4. Ignore 5. tempted

Abschlusstest

Übung 1: 1. Arianne, Maegan, Rhys, Caitlin and Owen
come from Wales.
2. He had captured Gareth and waited for
Arianne to try and rescue him.
3. Arianne is a musician and composer, Gareth is
an actor, Mary runs a B & B, Rhys had a shipping
company.
4. She thought there was no room for her, a
vampire, in his life in the limelight.

Übung 2:

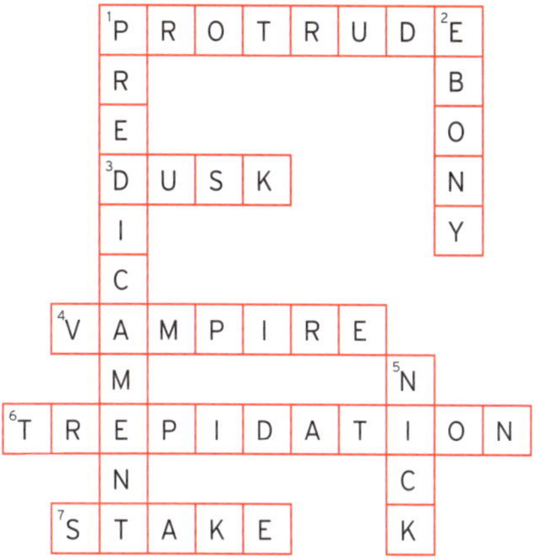
1 PROTRUDE
2 EBONY
PREDICAMENT
3 DUSK
4 VAMPIRE
5 NICK
6 TREPIDATION
7 STAKE

Übung 3: **1.** around, d **2.** out, e **3.** on, b **4.** up, a **5.** in, c

Übung 4: **1.** perch **2.** luscious **3.** snicker **4.** thrust

Übung 5: **1.** wraps **2.** wits **3.** cat got your tongue **4.** for the count

Übung 6: **1.** sich anschnallen, belt up **2.** trousers, pants
3. holiday(s), vacation **4.** snog, make out
5. bonnet, hood

Übung 7: **1.** Gareth has never visited Wales before.
2. Caitlin used to work for Arianne.
3. Mary lent Arianne a sword.
4. Maegan told Frederick a blatant lie.
5. Arianne was on the verge of tears.

Übung 8: **1.** evaporate **2.** abode **3.** limelight **4.** ripple **5.** bait
6. disrobe **7.** careen **8.** pensive
Lösung: vampires

Glossar

⚡ = umgangssprachlich

to abandon sth.	etw. aufgeben
abode	Bleibe
to accelerate	beschleunigen
agenda	*hier*: Absicht, Plan
agitation	Aufregung
all-consuming	alles verzehrend
all-terrain vehicle (ATV)	Geländewagen
ancestors *pl*	Vorfahren
to anticipate sth.	etw. erwarten
to arouse sth.	etw. erwecken, erregen
as the saying goes	wie es so schön heißt
awe	Ehrfurcht
backflip	Salto rückwärts
bait	Köder
bared	entblößt
to bask in sth.	etw. in vollen Zügen genießen
to be consumed by	verzehrt werden von
⚡ to be flabbergasted	völlig baff sein
to be in mourning	trauern
to belt up	sich anschnallen
to be one's own woman	eine selbstständige Frau sein
⚡ to be on the creepy side	ein wenig unheimlich sein
to be on the verge of sth.	am Rande von etw. stehen
⚡ to be out for the count	k.o. sein (bewusstlos)

to be stuck in a rut	im immer gleichen Trott gefangen sein
blankly	ausdruckslos
blatantly	offensichtlich, unverfroren
to blaze	(auf)lodern, glühen
blurry	verschwommen, unscharf
to blush	erröten
boneless	*hier*: total entspannt
to boot	obendrein, noch dazu
to bound	springen
to brace oneself for	sich gefasst machen auf
brusque	schroff, brüsk
⚡ bum leg (US)	kaputtes Bein
by mutual consent	in gegenseitigem Einverständnis
canopy bed	Himmelbett
captivating	faszinierend, bezaubernd
to careen	schlingern
to caress	streicheln, liebkosen
⚡ to catch on (to sth.)	etw. kapieren
causeway	Damm(straße)
to chastise sb.	jmd. schelten
⚡ chick	Tussi, Mieze
to chide sb.	jmd. tadeln
to chime	schlagen, läuten
clearing	Lichtung
to clear the air	reinen Tisch machen
club	*hier*: Keule
to comb	*hier*: durchkämmen, suchen
composer	Komponist(in)
to conceal sth.	etw. verstecken
condescending	herablassend
to confide sth. in sb.	jmd. etw. anvertrauen
to conquer sb.	jmd. besiegen
to counter	entgegnen, kontern
to cradle sb.	jmd. zärtlich halten

117

to crave sth.	etw. begehren
to creep (crept, crept)	kriechen
to crouch	(sich) kauern
cushy	bequem
dangling	baumelnd
to dash (out)	(heraus)stürmen, (heraus)rasen
dastardly	hinterhältig
to dawn on sb.	jmd. dämmern, jmd. aufgehen
dazzling	umwerfend, blendend
decay	Fäulnis, Verfall
deception	Täuschung, Betrug
delicate(ly)	sachte, zart
⚡ dense	dämlich
devastated	am Boden zerstört
disguise	Verkleidung
to dispose of sth.	etw. beseitigen
to disrobe	sich entkleiden
donor	(Blut-)Spender(in)
⚡ to do sb. in	jmd. kaltmachen
doting	(sehr) liebevoll, fürsorglich
double-edged	*hier*: mit zwei scharfen Enden
to drain sb.	*hier*: jmd. aussaugen
⚡ to drop a bombshell	eine Bombe platzen lassen
to drown out sth.	etw. übertönen
dusk	Abenddämmerung
to earn one's keep	seinen Lebensunterhalt verdienen
ebony	*hier*: tiefschwarz
eerie	unheimlich, gespenstisch
effortless(ly)	leicht, mühelos
to emerge from	herauskommen aus
enchantress	bezaubernde Frau, Zauberin
encroaching	sich ausbreitend
engagement	*hier*: Verlobung
to engulf sb.	jmd. überwältigen, verschlingen
ensuing	(nach)folgend

estate agency	Maklerbüro
to evaporate	sich in Luft auflösen, verdampfen
evasive	ausweichend
faint	schwach
to faint	in Ohnmacht fallen
to fall for sb.'s ruse	auf jds. List hereinfallen
⚡ to fall into sb.'s clutches	jmd. in die Hände fallen
fang	Reißzahn
fate	Schicksal
to fathom sth.	etw. begreifen
to feed (fed, fed) (on)	sich ernähren (von)
ferociously	wild
⚡ to floor the accelerator	Vollgas geben
⚡ fluke	glücklicher Zufall
to flutter	flattern
to foil sb.'s plans	jds. Pläne vereiteln
foolhardy	verwegen, töricht
for old times' sake	um der alten Zeiten willen
fragrant	duftend
frantically	verzweifelt, hektisch
free-for-all	(allgemeines) Gerangel
to fume	*hier*: vor Wut kochen
fuzzy	*hier*: benommen, benebelt
gag	*hier*: Knebel
to gasp	nach Luft schnappen, keuchen
gaze	Blick
to get the better of sb.	die Oberhand über jmd. gewinnen
to giggle	kichern
gingerly	vorsichtig
to give chase	verfolgen, hinterherrennen
to give sb. away	jmd. verraten
to give sth. a light squeeze	etw. sanft drücken
glee	Entzücken
⚡ to go bonkers	überschnappen
to go it alone	etw. im Alleingang machen

to graze	leicht berühren, streifen
grieving	trauernd
to groan	stöhnen
groin	Leistengegend
grove	Baumgruppe
growl	Knurren
⚡ hang-out	Treff, Stammlokal
⚡ Has the cat got your tongue?	Hat es dir die Sprache verschlagen?
⚡ to hatch a plan	einen Plan aushecken
to haunt sb.	jmd. heimsuchen, verfolgen
haven	Zufluchtsort
to head-butt sb.	jmd. einen Kopfstoß versetzen
heart-wrenching	herzzerreißend
heightened	geschärft, gesteigert
his nostrils flared	seine Nasenflügel bebten
hiss	Zischen
to howl	heulen, jaulen
to hurl	schleudern
if memory serves	wenn ich mich recht erinnere
ignition	Zündung
in a daze	benommen
inappropriate advances *pl*	unangemessene Annäherungs-versuche
incident	Ereignis
in earnest	richtig, ernsthaft
intertwined	(miteinander) verflochten
⚡ in the nick of time	gerade noch rechtzeitig
in the throes of desire	in Leidenschaft entbrannt
intimidating	bedrohlich, einschüchternd
intoxicating	berauschend
It's way past time.	Es ist allerhöchste Zeit.
to jackknife	eine Bewegung wie ein Klappmesser machen
to jerk	(herum)reißen
⚡ just sb.'s luck	Pech gehabt!

120

to keep one's wits about one	einen kühlen Kopf bewahren
to keep sb. out of harm's way	jmd. vor Schaden bewahren
⚡ to keep sth. under wraps	etw. unter Verschluss halten
to know no bounds	keine Grenzen kennen
languorously	wohlig, schläfrig
leap	Sprung, Satz
to leave sth. in one's wake	etw. hinter sich zurücklassen
leek	Lauch
lethal blow	Todesstoß
⚡ to let on that…	verraten, dass …
to let (let, let) up	nachlassen, aufhören
lilting	fröhlich, mit singendem Tonfall
limelight	Rampenlicht
longing	Sehnsucht, Verlangen
⚡ to look the worse for wear	lädiert aussehen
⚡ to lose (lost, lost) it	durchdrehen
lovebirds *pl*	Turteltauben
to lunge towards	sich stürzen auf
to lurk	lauern
luscious	sinnlich, voll
⚡ to make a beeline for sth.	schnurstracks auf etw. zulaufen
⚡ to make out (US)	(rum)knutschen, rummachen
malicious	boshaft, hasserfüllt
manor house	Landsitz, Herrenhaus
marble	Marmor
marital status	Familienstand
mate	*hier*: Gefährte/Gefährtin, Partner(in)
mesmerized	gebannt, wie hypnotisiert
⚡ miffed	verstimmt, verärgert
⚡ mind-boggling	irre, verrückt
to mingle with	sich (ver)mischen mit
to muffle	dämpfen
to murmur	murmeln
to neglect to do sth.	versäumen, etw. zu tun
nestled in	gekuschelt in

to niggle at	nagen an, beunruhigen
to no avail	vergeblich
to not add up	keinen Sinn ergeben
the odds are in sb.'s favour	jds. Chancen stehen nicht schlecht
outskirts *pl*	Stadtrand
to overwhelm sb.	jmd. überwältigen
oxygen	Sauerstoff
pace	Tempo
⚡ pal	Kumpel
pantry	Vorratskammer
to pass out	ohnmächtig werden
to peer	spähen, blicken
pensive	nachdenklich
to perch	hocken (auf)
to pick up on sb.'s trail	auf jds. Spur stoßen
pitch-dark	stockdunkel
to plead with sb.	jmd. anflehen
to plunge sth.	etw. stechen, rammen
⚡ to pop in	vorbeischauen
to pounce on sb.	über jmd. herfallen, sich auf jmd. stürzen
predator	Raubtier
predicament	Notlage
to probe	(nach)forschen
proprietress	Besitzerin
to protrude	herausragen
to provoke sb.	jmd. provozieren
to purr	schnurren
pursuit	Verfolgung
queasy	mulmig, übel
quest	Suche, Streben
to quiver	zittern
to rage	toben, wüten
to raise objections	Einwände erheben
ramification	Konsequenz

to rant	schimpfen, wettern
the rat race	ständiger Konkurrenzkampf
ravishing	hinreißend, atemberaubend
ray	Strahl
regal	majestätisch
reluctantly	widerwillig
to reproach oneself	sich Vorwürfe machen
revelation	Enthüllung
to rev up the engine	den Motor aufheulen lassen
to ripple	(sich) kräuseln
rugged features *pl*	markante Gesichtszüge
to rummage	(durch)wühlen
scanty	knapp
scent	Duft
to scold	schimpfen
score	*hier*: Filmmusik
to screech	quietschen
seductive(ly)	verführerisch
to send sb. on a wild goose chase	jmd. auf eine falsche Fährte locken
to settle a score	eine Rechnung begleichen
settlement	*hier*: Abfindung
shapely	wohlgeformt
should the worst come to the worst	wenn es ganz schlimm kommen sollte
shrub	Strauch
⚡ shut-eye	Schlaf, Nickerchen
sinister	finster, unheilvoll
sister-in-law	Schwägerin
to skewer	aufspießen
slumber	Schlummer
to snicker	spöttisch lachen
snide remark	abfällige Bemerkung
⚡ to snog (GB)	(rum)knutschen
⚡ to snoop (around)	(herum)schnüffeln

soothing	beruhigend
to spew	heraussprudeln, spritzen
spiked	stachelig, in Spitzen abstehend
to splinter	(zer)splittern
to stagger	wanken
stake	Pflock
⚡ to start (sth.) from scratch	(wieder) ganz von vorne anfangen
to stir	sich rühren, sich bewegen
stride	großer Schritt
stunned	fassungslos
succulent	wohlschmeckend, saftig
suspense	Spannung
to sweep (swept, swept)	*hier*: gleiten
tabloid	Boulevardzeitung
teasing	neckend
⚡ to tell sb. where to get off	jmd. was husten, jmd. ordentlich Bescheid sagen
tempting	verlockend, verführerisch
tentatively	zögernd
⚡ thick	begriffsstutzig
throbbing	pochend
to thrust (thrust, thrust)	stoßen
tinged with	mit einer Spur von
tinted	getönt
to tip sb. off	jmd. einen Hinweis geben
to toss around sth.	etw. hin und her werfen
touchy	heikel, empfindlich
trained on	gerichtet auf
⚡ to traipse	latschen
trepidation	Beklommenheit
triple harp	(walisische) Tripelharfe
⚡ to tuck into	verschlingen, zulangen
to tug	zerren, reißen
turmoil	Tumult
to turn the tables	den Spieß umdrehen

under sb.'s thumb	unter jds. Fuchtel
unruly	widerspenstig
untamed	wild, ungebändigt
unwittingly	unbeabsichtigterweise
upholstered	gepolstert
upkeep	Instandhaltung
uproar	Aufruhr
urge	Drang
vamp	Verführerin, Vamp
vantage point	Aussichtspunkt
vicious	bösartig, grausam
the Victorian Age	das viktorianische Zeitalter (1837-1901)
to vow	geloben
⚡ wallop	Rums, (harter) Schlag
whiff	Hauch, Spur
to whimper	wimmern
white lie	Notlüge
⚡ to whizz by	vorbeifliegen
wicked(ly)	boshaft
winded	außer Atem
to wipe sb.'s memory	jds. Erinnerungen löschen
with all one's might	mit aller Kraft
to worship	anbeten
to wrench sth.	etw. (mit einem Ruck) reißen
to wrest sth. from sb.	jmd. etw. entreißen
to writhe	sich winden
wrought-iron	schmiedeeisern
wry	trocken, ironisch
to yank off	(ruckartig) abreißen

Verzeichnis der Übungen

Abschlusstest

Mehr Sprachen – noch mehr Gänsehaut

Lesespaß mit Lerneffekt!

Weitere Titel:

Englisch, B1, 6,95 €
ISBN 978-3-8174-7950-4

Englisch, B1, 6,95 €
ISBN 978-3-8174-7951-1

Englisch, B2, 6,95 €
ISBN 978-3-8174-7952-8

Englisch, B2, 6,95 €
ISBN 978-3-8174-7953-5

Englisch, C1, 8,95 €
ISBN 978-3-8174-8261-0

Englisch, C1, 8,95 €
ISBN 978-3-8174-8262-7

Spanisch, B1, 6,95 €
ISBN 978-3-8174-8264-1

Französisch, B1, 6,95 €
ISBN 978-3-8174-8263-4

Jeder Band 128 Seiten, zweifarbig, Broschur, Format 12,5 x 19 cm
Ab Frühjahr 2011 auch für Italienisch erhältlich!

„Eine ideale Kombination – mit Genuss schmökern und so
die Fremdsprachenkenntnisse ganz nebenbei verbessern."

Weitere Lernlektüren unter:
www.compactverlag.de | www.lernkrimi.de